THE NOBLE BEREAN
VOLUME 3

...AND THEY SEARCHED THE SCRIPTURES DAILY,
WHETHER THOSE THINGS WERE SO...

by

Thomas M. Kissinger

Straightway Publishing Company

Baton Rouge, Louisiana

The Noble Berean Series Volume 3

The Noble Berean:
And They Searched The Scriptures Daily,
Whether Those Things Were So

Copyright © 2011 by Thomas M. Kissinger
Straightway Publishing Company

All rights reserved. Any passage, except quotes, may be reproduced in any form whatsoever without permission from the author. All Scripture quotations are from the King James Version of the Bible unless otherwise noted.

For further information, contact the author through Straightway Publishing Company

Published by:
Straightway Publishing Company
Post Office Box 45212 #261
Baton Rouge, LA. 70895
Email: tkissinger01@cox.net
(225) 766-0896

Book and cover design: Rich Baldwin

The Noble Berean:
And They Searched The Scriptures Daily,
Whether Those Things Were So

By Thomas M. Kissinger

1. Author 2. Title 3. Inspiration 4. Religion
Library of Congress Control Number: 2007904055
ISBN: 978-0-9785134-3-6 (Paperback)

Printed in the United States of America

To my wife Sarah, and our children Moriah, Makayla, and Micah. My love for each of you grows every day. You are the four most precious things I have been given the privilege of experiencing in this life. I would have no life or even a reason to write without you. You are my inspiration and the very expression of God's love, grace, and mercy. May each one of you receive **The Revelation of Jesus Christ! May you personally know Him - Who He is, and what He has accomplished for the human race!**

To Louis Thompson. You are the greatest man of God I know. Your drive to seek first the Kingdom of God and His righteousness is incredible. Thank you for infecting me with a burning desire to know Who God is and what He has accomplished. You are a walking epistle and testimony to the reality of **God's Revelation Truth!**

To Billy Thompson. Where would I be without all your instruction, patience, and teaching? You have "rightly divided" to me the reconciliation of all things through Jesus Christ. You are a magnificent friend with a magnificent gift. I can always count on you to be there for me!

To Dr. Harold Lovelace. We are all indebted to you for the pioneer trail you have blazed for many decades now. You have given me the "key of knowledge" and unlocked the door to the **Holy Mysteries of Almighty God!**

To Dr. Stephen Jones. I cannot thank you enough for sharing your writings and insight concerning God's Kingdom with the world. How liberating it is to understand the process of our personal salvation spirit, soul, and body, as well as **God's Three Harvests** of souls which will result in the restoration of all things. Remarkable…well done! Your writings stand alone!

To Pastor David Davis. Thank you and Sharon for your faithfulness and love. You both remain diligent and committed to your calling, in that you understand, teach, and live the Christ-Life. We are all grateful for having been taught about the true **Abiding Hope** that resides within!

To Chris Dantin. You are a breath of fresh air and a tremendous encouragement. Your eye-opening experience concerning God's sovereignty, love, and salvation for all, including your willingness to express gratitude to those who brought this information to you, is astounding. You have not shunned to declare what has been revealed to you. This is the mark of a true disciple of Jesus Christ and evidence that you are a genuine Berean.

You have searched the Scriptures daily to see if the things you have been taught through the years are so. Well done, my friend! You will be one that God uses mightily!

To Rich Baldwin. Your level of talent concerning design is nothing short of phenomenal. It is a beautiful thing how the Lord brought us together as friends through this whole process. You do excellent work!

To Thomas and Nancy St.Amant. It has been said that, "A friend loves at all times, and a brother is born for adversity." It is no secret that you two are our closest and dearest friends, but I just want to thank you for your friendship. You have helped us through some very tough, lonely, and dark times. We cherish our relationship with you!

To Mary Cage. You have been such a huge part of all that I have been able to accomplish. Without your help there would be no websites, books, or recordings available through me. I really do not have the proper vocabulary to let you know just how much you mean to me. Once again, thank you from the bottom of my heart for your many hours of editing!

GRAND STATEMENT

*…they received the word with all readiness of mind,
and searched the Scriptures daily,
whether those things were so.*

Acts 17:11

To all those who are Bereans at heart. I appreciate you
for your willingness to receive God's Word with all readiness
of mind. Continue to search the Scriptures daily!

To all those who are yet to be Bereans.
You are invited to take a journey to the heart
of the one and true living God!

INTRODUCTION

The following words are from a letter I received from Eulene Moores. Her kind words were so encouraging and such an honor that I thought they were fitting to serve as the introduction of this book. Eulene and her husband David live in Alberta, Canada. Eulene is also a writer and has a website which contains her writings. Her website is: www.lettersofhope.org.

Dear Brother Thomas,

"I have finished reading both of the Noble Berean books and want to tell you that so much of what the Lord has taught me through my seven decades of walking with Him has been expertly distilled and confirmed in these books.

Your insights and your expression of such wonderful Scriptural truths are appreciated, and I thank you for sharing what God has revealed to you of His sovereignty and His intentional purpose for the whole of His glorious creation.

We are now "standing on tiptoe" awaiting the revealing of His sons and the deliverance they will bring to the world in His soon-coming Kingdom, and we are "pressing on to lay hold…"

God bless you as you continue to serve Him in all to which He has called you."

In Christ's Love,

Eulene Moores

CONTENTS

PART 1 - THE THREE HARVESTS

PART 2 - WHAT IS TRUTH?

PART 3 - BLIND FROM BIRTH

PART 4 - LEARNING OBEDIENCE

PART 5 - HOW SAY SOME AMONG YOU THERE IS NO RESURRECTION OF THE DEAD?

PART 6 - GOD'S SOVEREIGNTY AND MAN'S AUTHORITY

PART 7 - ELITE VS. ELECT

PART 8 - POPULAR OBJECTIONS TO THE RECONCILIATION OF ALL THINGS (Part 1)

PART 9 - POPULAR OBJECTIONS TO THE RECONCILIATION OF ALL THINGS (Part 2)

PART 10 - THE MAN WITH THE BOOTS

PART 1 - THE THREE HARVESTS: BARLEY, WHEAT, AND GRAPES

One of the great gifts that God has given to mankind is the ability to express ourselves through the avenue of writing. Writing allows us to take all of our beliefs, visions, thoughts, hopes, and dreams and to spell them out in a way that they can be read, viewed, and preserved for generations to come. Unfortunately, though, one of the disadvantages of writing is that we are only able to write, explain, and elaborate on particular topics to the degree we understand them at that point in time. As time goes on, we will naturally find better ways to say things, even discovering that we may need to adjust, amend, or modify some of the things which we have already written and put in print.

Throughout my writings I refer to the Feasts of Passover, Pentecost, and Tabernacles that are mentioned in the Bible, and how they symbolically refer to our salvation on the individual level as well as God's three harvests of souls on the corporate level. The three harvests that the Bible speaks of are: Barley, Wheat, and Grapes. In addition to all of this, I have written that these three harvests represent a "remnant" (overcomers), "the nations", and "the world in general" (including the church in general and all unbelievers). It is this last statement that I wish to modify and bring more clarity to.

After further research I have come to understand the three harvests (Barley, Wheat, and Grapes) which we have mentioned in a greater and more specific way. In previous writings I have assigned the Barley, Wheat, and Grape Harvests to: Overcomers, The Nations, and The World In General. In a sense, this is correct, but I have discovered through the writings of Dr. Stephen Jones a better and more perfect way to rightly divide and explain these three great harvests.

The Barley Harvest represents the first part of God's harvest. Those in this first harvest are referred to in Scripture as "overcomers". The gathering in of the **nations** is actually a *result* of the Barley Harvest. It is in and through the manifestation of the sons of God that all nations will come to know the Lord and serve Him. These "overcomers" shall come forth in the first resurrection to rule and reign on the earth under the leadership of the Lord Jesus Christ!

The Wheat Harvest represents "the church in general". It speaks of those who were justified by faith, but either did not go through or submit to the sanctification process of the Lord. They are believers, but are in need of further correction in order to be fully sanctified and put on the divine nature and character of their Heavenly Father. There still remains **iniquity (lawlessness)** in their lives that must be purged by the fire (the fiery law) of God. Those who are part of the Wheat Harvest shall be brought forth in the second resurrection to be saved *"yet so as through fire"* (1 Cor. 3:15).

The Grape Harvest represents "the unbelievers". It speaks of those who have neither been justified nor sanctified. They shall go through God's wrath, judgment, and the lake of fire for the purpose of correction.

The Good News to be associated with all of this is that these three harvests represent and guarantee the salvation of all in the fullness of time. As far as God is concerned, salvation for all is not "if", but "when". Let us call to remembrance what Paul told us in 1st Corinthians 15:22-23, which states…

‍²²For as in Adam all die, so also in Christ all shall be made alive. ²³But each in his own order [tagma, "squadron"].

Here are some excerpts and quotes from the writings of Dr. Stephen Jones to support the things which have been stated. The quotes were taken from his writings entitled "Creation's Jubilee" and "The Restoration Of All Things". They are from various spots throughout these written works.

According to Dr. Stephen Jones:

"If we were to study the passages in the Bible where barley is mentioned, we would find much valuable information about the first resurrection and the character and calling of those who qualify for it. The fact that barley matures early tells us that the "barley firstfruits" are the first people to mature spiritually to bring forth the fruits of the kingdom that God requires. Barley also can survive drought, heat, and cold much more easily than can wheat.

The Church in general will be raised in the second resurrection. Jesus calls them "the just" who receive Life at the same time "the unjust" are judged at the beginning of that final age in the lake of fire. In either case, the fire that judges is the same fire poured out on Pentecost. God's judgment is designed to *"thoroughly clear His threshing floor; and He will gather His wheat into the barn"* (Matthew 3:12).

The baptism of fire upon the wheat (Church) is both good and bad. It represents a purification process, which is judgment upon sin in order to bless the individual. When God works to refine or purify someone, it is not a pleasant experience. No judgment is. But those who understand the mind and purpose of God will readily submit to His fire, knowing that God is working all things out for their good.

Finally, a Biblical study of the grape harvest, with the treading of the grapes in the winepresses, tells us the fate of the unbelievers. The winepress depicts God's wrath, judgment, and the lake of fire.

The purpose of the grain harvests of spring (barley and wheat) is to provide bread for God's great communion table. The purpose of the Feast of Tabernacles with its celebration of the winepress is to provide the wine for God's table. Without this wine, His communion table would have only bread and would be incomplete. God will have His wine, but it must come by means of the winepress, which speaks of the judgments of God.

God harvests His barley, wheat, and grapes in different manners, even as nature teaches us. The chaff from the barley falls away very easily, so barley is said to be *winnowed*. That is, the action of the wind itself (by means of fans) are sufficient to get rid of the chaff. This speaks of the barley company, who so quickly respond to the wind of the Spirit.

To remove the chaff from the wheat requires threshing. This is a more severe action, but it does the job. It depicts the fact that the Church will be harvested by means of judgment, or tribulation. The Latin word, *tribulum*, is a threshing instrument.

Finally, to obtain the juice the grapes must be trodden under foot. Grapes do not have chaff, but they do have "flesh" that must be pressed severely in order to obtain the wine. This represents the most severe form of judgment upon the unbelievers. Yet the result is that God obtains wine for His communion table." -end quote- (Creation's Jubilee, Dr. Stephen Jones)

According to Dr. Stephen Jones:

"There is more than one resurrection coming. The first "squadron" will be those who are called to rule and reign with Him (Rev. 20:4-6). The second group will be those believers who are raised along with all the unbelievers (John 5:28, 29; Luke 12:46) at the Great White Throne (Rev. 20:11-13). This second group of believers will miss the first resurrection and will not reign with Christ during the thousand years in the Tabernacles Age to come. Nonetheless, they will certainly be *"saved yet so as through fire"* (1 Cor. 3:15). Jesus made it clear in Luke 12:46-49 that those servants of God who mistreated others would receive a "flogging" before being given their reward.

The third group will be the unbelievers themselves, after their time of judgment has been completed, for there will be a Jubilee at the end of time according to the law, wherein all of creation will be set free in the glorious liberty of the children of God (Rom. 8:21)." -end quote-(<u>The Restoration Of All Things</u>, Dr. Stephen Jones)

PART 2 - WHAT IS *TRUTH*?

In the eighteenth chapter of the Gospel of John we are taken through a series of events that set the stage for one of the most dramatic questions in all of history. The chapter starts out with the betrayal of Jesus by Judas, which then leads to the arrest of Jesus (by a band of men and officers from the chief priests) in the Garden of Gethsemane. Before this arrest takes place, though, we become aware (in dramatic fashion) of the manifested power of the Son of God as He identifies Himself as: I AM HE! John goes on to tell us…that as Jesus referred to Himself in this way (I AM HE), that those present went backward and fell to the ground. This testifies to the power and reality of Who Jesus the Christ was and is: The Great I AM (Divinity and Deity clothed and manifested in human flesh). The first passage of the chapter ends with the zealous act of Peter, as he grabs a sword and cuts off the right ear of one of the high priest's servants. The Gospel of Luke informs us, though, that Jesus touched his ear, and healed him (Luke 22:51). Jesus always took time to demonstrate his miracle-working power, mercy, and compassion to others, even as He was being falsely accused and arrested unjustly.

 From this point on the King of kings is bound like a common criminal and led away to stand before Annas first, and then to appear before

Caiaphas, who was the high priest. It is at this point in the chapter that the scene changes and we are suddenly made aware of Peter being confronted by a damsel about his supposed association with Jesus. We are told that Peter followed Jesus, and so did another disciple. The other disciple went in with Jesus into the place of the high priest, but Peter stood at the door without. As Peter was questioned by the damsel that kept the door, he denied that he was one of the disciples of Jesus. He would later go on to deny Jesus two more times. Let us not be too hard on Peter, though, for we have all denied Jesus in our lives at one time or another. As we all know, Peter went on to be one of the greatest men of God who ever lived and was the one to write of God's divine nature in 2nd Peter chapter one.

JESUS AND THE HIGH PRIEST

As we continue on our journey through John chapter eighteen, pressing toward *the question of questions*, we now find Jesus before the high priest (after being led to Annas first) being grilled as to the nature of His disciples and doctrine. Rather than defending Himself, He answers His accusers (as usual) in a way that causes them to look within, even making use of a question to answer their question. Jesus asks and states in John 18:21..."Why do you ask Me? Ask them which heard Me, what I have said unto them: behold, they know what I said." Enraged with the answer Jesus gave (because it was a non-direct and intelligent answer that turned the heat back on the high priest), we are told that one of the officers which stood by struck Jesus in the face with the palm of his hand. Once again, it is not recorded that Jesus retaliated verbally or physically in any way, but that He calmly answered the man who struck Him as to why He responded to the high priest in that manner. In the Gospel of Matthew we are told that Jesus was asked directly whether or not He was the Christ, the Son of God. The answer Jesus gave to the high priest (you shall see the Son of Man sitting on the right hand of power, and coming in the clouds of heaven) provoked a rather violent response from the listeners. They accused Him of blasphemy, which, according to the Jews was that Jesus -- being a man -- claimed and made Himself to be God (John 10:33) by calling Himself the Christ, the Son of God.

In the Gospel of Mark, when asked by the high priest if He was the Christ, the Son of the Blessed, Jesus said...I AM. Any who are familiar with the Old Testament know that the words I AM are a direct reference to Jehovah (God), and that He revealed Himself to Moses as...I AM THAT I AM! In essence, these words were perceived by the Jews as a claim to be God, and so they should have, for this is exactly Who Jesus was and is. He is the Word (God) Who was made flesh, and dwelled among us (John 1:1; John 1:14). Oh what our Lord endured next as some spit on Him, blindfolded Him, and struck Him with their fists, saying to Him, "Prophesy!" After that, the guards took Him and beat Him. **What a picture of love and humility as Jesus received this (having done nothing wrong) at the hands of those who were actually sinners in need of Him as their Savior! He opened not His mouth in accusation against them! In essence, Jesus became a <u>creditor</u>, in that He was an innocent victim, falsely accused, and treated harshly. The KEY is that He did not open His mouth to defend Himself or retaliate, but rather, He <u>FORGAVE</u> those who acted out against Him in ignorance and violence.**

According to Dr. Stephen Jones:

"In fact, an overcomer is one who overcomes something. Without something to overcome, how can he be an overcomer? The only way one can exercise the power of forgiveness is to have something to forgive. To have something to forgive, one must be a victim of some sort of sin. No one is called to forgive an act of kindness." -end quote- (<u>How To Be An Overcomer</u>, Dr. Stephen Jones)

In reference to all of this, Isaiah so eloquently prophesied of the events which would take place concerning Jesus (His suffering and death on our behalf). Isaiah chapter fifty-three is one of the most remarkable prophecies concerning Jesus as *The Suffering Servant*. Isaiah 53:3-7 states…"He is despised and rejected of men; a man of sorrows, and acquainted with grief: and we hid as it were our faces from Him; He was despised, and we esteemed Him not. Surely He has borne our griefs, and carried our sorrows: yet we did esteem Him stricken, smitten of God, and afflicted. But He was wounded for our transgressions, He was bruised for our iniquities: the chastisement of our peace was upon Him; and with His stripes we are healed. All we like sheep have gone astray; we have turned every one to his own way; and the LORD has laid on Him the iniquity of us all. He was oppressed, and He was afflicted, **yet He opened not His mouth**: He is brought as a lamb to the slaughter, and as a sheep before her shearers is dumb, **so He opened not His mouth**." Take the time to read all of Isaiah chapter fifty-three to see how explicit and precise Isaiah's prophecy was concerning Christ. Jesus applied this prophecy to Himself (Luke 22:37), as did His disciples (Matthew 8:17; John 12:38; Hebrews 9:28; Revelation 5:6, 12; 13:8).

JESUS AND PONTIUS PILATE

To recap the series of events that brought Jesus to His meeting with Pontius Pilate, let us state for the record: First, He was taken to the house of Annas; then, the meeting with Caiaphas and the Sanhedrin; then, to Pilate; and then to Herod before finally being brought back to Pilate again. In Luke 23:8-12, it is said that Herod was glad to see Jesus because he had heard many things of Him and hoped to have seen some miracle done by Him. After much questioning, and Jesus answering nothing, the chief priests and scribes stood and vehemently accused Him. Before being led back to Pilate again, Jesus was mocked and ridiculed, being arrayed in a gorgeous robe. It is interesting to note that the events which took place before Herod are only recorded in the Gospel of Luke, and that Pilate and Herod were made friends together: for before that day they were enemies. With all this being said, let us now go back to the initial meeting of Jesus and Pilate as it is recorded in the Gospel of John.

According to Wikipedia, The Free Encyclopedia:

"**Pontius Pilate** was the Equestrian procurator (Roman governor) of the Roman province of Judaea from AD 26-36. Typically referenced as the fifth Procurator of Judea, he is best known as the judge at Jesus' trial and the man who authorized His crucifixion.

Pilate appears in all four canonical Christian Gospels. Mark, depicting Jesus as innocent of plotting against Rome, portrays Pilate as extremely reluctant to execute Jesus, blaming the Jewish priestly hierarchy for His death. In Matthew, Pilate washes his hands of Jesus and reluctantly sends Him to His death. In Luke, Pilate not only agrees that Jesus did not conspire against Rome, but Herod Antipas, the tetrarch, also finds nothing treasonous in Jesus' actions. In John, Jesus' claim to be the Son of Man or the Messiah to Pilate and the Sanhedrin is not portrayed at all…

According to Philo (a Jewish philosopher), Pilate was "inflexible, he was stubborn, of cruel disposition. He executed troublemakers without a trial." He refers to Pilate's "venality, his violence, thefts, assaults, abusive behavior, endless executions, endless savage ferocity."

According to Josephus (a Jewish historian), Pilate repeatedly almost caused insurrections among the Jews due to his insensitivity to Jewish customs. While Pilate's predecessors had respected Jewish customs by removing all images and effigies on their standards when entering Jerusalem, Pilate allowed his soldiers to bring them into the city at night." -end quote- (Pontius Pilate, Wikipedia, The Free Encyclopedia)

As the scene changes and Jesus is brought unto the hall of judgment, it is this man (the inflexible, stubborn, cruel, and insensitive Pilate) whom the Lord of glory (Jesus) finds Himself standing before. It is said that the name "Pilate" means "armed with a spear". It is common knowledge that a spear is used to pierce someone or something. With this in mind, it is safe to say that Pilate was an instrument of God who was about to be used to "pierce" the very heart of the mission of the Lord Jesus Christ, exposing to all and for all time the nature and goal of the coming of the Son of God, the King of the Jews.

Jesus is now led from Caiaphas unto the hall of judgment. We are told that it was early; and they themselves went not into the judgment hall, lest they should be defiled; but that they might eat the Passover. How ironic that those who falsely accused Jesus of blasphemy were concerned about being defiled, not knowing that Jesus was the True Passover Lamb of God Who came to take away the sin of the world. He (Jesus) was the cure for their defilement, but they were not able to perceive or grasp the hour of their visitation. Was it not the apostle John who also enlightened us as to the nature of the coming of Jesus and His rejection when he stated in John 1:5 and John 1:11…"And the light shines in the darkness; and the darkness comprehended it not…He came unto His own, and His own received Him not."

Pilate then went out to them, and said, "What accusation do you bring against this man?" Now remember…Pilate was not the slightest bit interested in the Jews, their preachers, or their prophets. One gets the feeling he was quite nauseated at the thought of having to deal with this matter and would have rather been anywhere else doing just about anything but being called into the ring to referee another one of the Jews' religious quarrels. As historians have documented, Pilate was notorious for being sarcastic, insensitive, unmoved, indifferent, and quite irritated (to say the least) when it came to Jewish beliefs, rituals, and customs. This caused the accusers of Jesus, to all the more, defend their position and justify their reasons for delivering up (in their opinion) this malefactor (one who commits an offense against the law).

After hearing the Jews plead with him concerning their desire to see Jesus condemned, Pilate makes his first attempt to wash his hands of this bothersome situation, asking the Jews to take *their Jesus* and judge Him according to *their law*. It is at this moment that the true motive of the Jews is brought to light, as they reveal their intentions to have Jesus put to death. They answer Pilate by saying in John 18:31…"It is not lawful for us to put any man to death." Once Pilate realizes he is not going to be able to convince the Jews to handle this matter on their own, it is said he entered into the judgment hall again and called Jesus, asking Him about His claim of being a king with a kingdom. What transpires next is some of the most interesting and exciting dialogue in all of Scripture, climaxing with *the question of questions*, which all have pondered in their hearts at one time or another down through history.

"Are You the King of the Jews?" Pilate asked Jesus. Wow…you talk about a loaded question! It is at this moment that Jesus takes "the spear" of Pilate, turns it around, and pierces Pilate's heart, and all others for that matter. It has never ceased to amaze and fascinate me how Jesus was the Master at answering a question with another penetrating question that caused the listener to reflect and look within. According to the Amplified Bible, Jesus answered and said…"Are you saying this of yourself [on your own initiative], or have others told you about Me?" (John 18:34) This is an important question due to the fact that it penetrates the heart of the listeners, causing them to examine themselves and where they stand on the issue of: Who is Jesus? This scene should also remind us of the two times Jesus asked His disciples, saying, "Whom do men say that I the Son of Man am?" And later…He asked them in a more personal way, saying, "But Whom say *you* that I am?" (Matthew 16:13-15)

In other words, Jesus was asking Pilate (and all others for that matter) if he (Pilate) really wanted to know Who He (Jesus) was, or would he (Pilate) just settle for repeating what others had told him, not having any true understanding or revelation for himself. From this point on in the conversation we find ourselves present at a *"showdown at high noon"* of two forces *"slappin' leather"*! The two forces I am speaking of are not Jesus and Pilate, for Pilate was only a puppet in the situation and no match for the Master. These two opposing forces engaged in battle are: Jesus / <u>Revelation Truth</u> *vs.* <u>Religion</u> / religious rhetoric spoken by men who have no understanding of what they say. This has always been the battle down through the ages. It is a battle for "the minds of men". Do you remember what the apostle Paul stated in 2nd Corinthians 4:3-4? He said…"But if our gospel be hid, it is hid to them that are lost: In whom **the god of this world has blinded the minds** of them which believe not, lest the light of the glorious gospel of <u>Christ, Who is the image of God</u>, should shine unto them."

Well…It was not Pilate's time to be enlightened or to have the blinders taken off of his mind by the Spirit of God as this scene unfolds. All of these things were foretold and prophesied, which meant that Jesus had to be crucified to take away the sin of the world. Pilate then sarcastically spouts off, answering Jesus by saying, "Am I a Jew? Your own nation and the chief priests have delivered You unto me: what have You done?" (John 18:35) *Oh my*…this is another loaded question. **What has Jesus done?** Can you imagine if Jesus really had taken the time to properly answer Pilate according to this question? Surely Jesus would still be giving the answer today as we attempt to capture this great moment in history. Jesus probably did not answer Pilate directly due to what John wrote about Him in his Gospel, when he stated, "And there are also many other things which Jesus did, the which, if they should be written every one, I suppose that even **the world itself could not contain the books that should be written**. Amen." (John 21:25)

Well…since Pilate asked the question (What have You done?), let's take a moment to reflect on some of the high points of what our Jesus has done. Here are just some of the things Jesus has done:

- Created the heaven and the earth…

- Used Noah and the Ark to cleanse the world…

- Called Abram and promised that through him all families of the earth will be blessed…

- Revealed Himself as the God of Abraham, Isaac, and Jacob…

- Raised up Joseph to rule the world in his day…

- Revealed Himself to Moses as…I AM THAT I AM…

- Used Moses to deliver His people from the mighty Pharaoh of Egypt…

- Gave us the Law…

- Brought His people through the wilderness and into the Promised Land…

- Raised up Judges, Prophets, and Kings to deliver His people…

- Became flesh and dwelled among us (Emmanuel / God with us)…

- Revealed Himself as a King, Servant, Man, and God…

- Preached the Gospel, healed the brokenhearted,
  preached deliverance to the captives, opened blinded eyes,
  set at liberty the bruised, performed miracles,
  healed the sick, and raised the dead…

- Died on the Cross to take away the sin of the *world*…

- Rose again to defeat death for *all*…

- Gave us the apostles and Paul who revealed
  the New Covenant…

- Gave us access to the baptism and infilling of His Holy Spirit…

- Promised to come again through His people
  (the manifestation of the sons of God) to deliver
  the creation from bondage and corruption, until
  all things are restored and reconciled back to the Father…

As we stated earlier, Jesus does not answer Pilate directly concerning the specific question He was asked. Instead, Jesus begins to speak heavenly things from the Spirit realm as to Who He is, where He came from, and what He has come here to accomplish. Surely Pilate must have thought he was hearing *gibberish* and *nonsense* coming from the lips of the Master when Jesus answered him and said, "My kingdom is not of this world: if My kingdom were of this world, then would My servants fight, that I should not be delivered to the Jews: but now is My kingdom not from here." (John 18:36) I do believe, though, after hearing an answer of this nature that Pilate begins to suspect there is something very different and unique about this man named Jesus, and that Pilate at this point is actually mesmerized, waiting to hear what things Jesus will say next.

For those of you who are reading this, please excuse me for just a moment as I speculate on the emotion and drama of what is about to transpire next between Pontius Pilate and The World's Redeemer. Whereas Pilate first looked at Jesus as a non-issue and inconsequential, he now is fascinated at the brazen boldness of this man Who claims to be a king and in possession of a kingdom. Pilate thinks to himself, "How can this man possibly claim to be a king with a kingdom, but in actuality His outward appearance is one of weakness, and there is no such external evidence whatsoever to support His ludicrous claim?" But nevertheless, Pilate (for a brief moment in time) is held spellbound as to how Jesus will answer him from this point on. The look on Pilate's face now changes to that of being stunned, puzzled, and bewildered, but also coupled with excitement, expectation, and intrigue.

Once again, Pilate goes back to his original question and interest in whether or not Jesus sees Himself and proclaims Himself to be a king. Pilate seems to be thinking to himself, "I refuse to leave this situation unless I am able to get this man to answer me as to whether He sees Himself as a king or not!" Of all the wild and crazy cases in which Pilate has found himself responsible for passing judgment, this has turned out to be the most captivating one of all, and Pilate has now invested himself and wants a return for pouring his soul and time into this matter. In order to satisfy his curiosity, Pilate asks Jesus again if He is a king. Jesus then answers him and reveals the purpose of His mission on earth. Their conversation climaxes when Pilate asks Jesus *the question of questions*.

Here is how John 18:37-38 reads in the Amplified Bible…"Then You are a King? Jesus answered, you say it! [You speak correctly!] For I am a King. [Certainly I am a King!] **This is why I was born, and for this I have come into the world, to bear witness to the _Truth_. Everyone who is of the _Truth [who is a friend of the Truth, who belongs to the Truth]_ hears and listens to My voice.** Pilate said to Him, _What is Truth?_ On saying this he went out to the Jews again and told them, I find no fault in Him."

After Pilate asks Jesus whether He is a king and hears His response, he (Pilate) asks Him one more question. In my opinion, this is a question for the ages, and probably one of the most important questions of all time, if not *the most important question* ever asked. As he asks Jesus this question the look on Pilate's face is one of confusion. Pilate is not quite sure what to think at this instant. His initial thought is to be sarcastic, but on the tail end of this emotion he is actually hoping for Jesus to give him an answer. For a split second Pilate forgets who he is and where he is and gets lost in the majesty of standing before the King of kings. The three words (**_What is truth?_**) leave Pilate's lips and everyone in the room cannot believe what they are hearing. The moment is surreal. The level of expectation and tension among those who are present is beyond anything else in history. The stage is set. *The question of questions* has been asked. The "spear of Pilate" has been thrust into the heart, mission, and purpose of the Savior. It is so quiet one can hear a pin drop. It is all too much to capture in print. **Oh the wonder of it all!**

All of us know full well that Jesus could have answered Pilate's question to the degree that Pilate and all those in the room would have recognized Him as the Savior of the world and bowed down to Him in worship. But it was not according to the purpose of God at that time due to the fact Jesus had to die on the cross for the sin of the world. For this reason, Jesus does not open His mouth, and in turn, seals His fate of crucifixion. Pilate, who still finds no fault in Jesus, mumbles under his breath, "This man is no threat, just a foolish dreamer." Pilate says this with a certain amount of disappointment; for once again, he really was hoping to hear a response from Jesus concerning…***What is truth?***

After this, Pilate gets creative in an effort to find a way to pardon Jesus by offering to uphold a Jewish custom at the Passover, which consists of releasing one prisoner. He offers to release Jesus - The King of the Jews. Shockingly enough, the people insist to have Barabbas, who is a thief, released instead. With this being said, John chapter eighteen comes to an end, but our discussion does not. Thanks to Pilate we are now left with probably the greatest question ever asked in the annals of history, which is: ***What is truth?***

WHAT IS TRUTH?

For many, the initial question in this line of thinking is: Is there any such thing as *truth*?…or…Does *truth* exist? Upon hearing from those who are atheistic or agnostic, we could expect to hear such answers as: No…I don't care…I don't think so…I don't believe in God or *truth*…and so on. For those who have been born of the Spirit of the living God, though, we know and believe in *"truth"*. It is **impossible** to deny what has been revealed to us through our experience in the **Word of God**, the **Spirit of God**, the **Anointing**, and our relationship with **Jesus Christ** - the Word, Spirit, and Anointing made flesh; the One Who dwelled among us to be the visible manifestation and demonstration of *truth*.

Before we attempt to define *truth*, though, let us state for the record what *truth* is not. It is not any particular religious gathering, cult, denomination, or non-denominational organization. As a matter of fact, it is not an organization at all. In addition to this, it is not a religion, such as the Catholic Church. The more you try to organize *truth* according to men's organizational standards, the more watered down it becomes, as those in charge allow their ideas and the traditions and doctrines of men to creep in. *Truth* is not a set of rules and regulations, where you or I "go to church", or who our pastor or priest is; and it is definitely not the *mindset* of what the majority of those in Christianity, who espouse false doctrine concerning the person and work of Jesus Christ, think it is. To the surprise of many, it is none of these things we have mentioned. Well...***What is truth?*** I am so glad you asked! Let us now give due diligence to this *question of questions* as we once again become a *Noble Berean*, searching the Scriptures daily in pursuit of the knowledge of Christ.

TO THIS END / FOR THIS CAUSE

Have you ever stopped and wondered about the coming of the Lord? Why was He born? Why did He come? What was His purpose and mission? What was His true cause? Why did He die? Why did He **have** to die? How did we "get lost", which in turn created the need for us to "be saved"? If Jesus came to save us, then what did He save us from, and why? These are the types of questions we need to ask ourselves and others. They are deep, probing and penetrating questions that (when the answers are discovered) will bring deliverance to the soul. Looking back on the response of Jesus to Pilate concerning whether He (Jesus) was a king or not, Jesus replied, "You say that I am a king. **To this end was I born, and for this cause came I into the world, that I should bear witness unto the** *truth*. Every one that is of the *truth* hears My voice." (John 18:37) Well...there you have it! There is "The Answer" we are looking for. It is all about the *truth*, and this is the very reason why Jesus was born, lived, died for the sin of the world, and rose again. It was all to BEAR WITNESS UNTO THE *TRUTH*!

The word *"truth"* used by Jesus in this passage comes from the Greek word "aletheia". This simply means: **unveiled reality**. It can also be referred to as **revelation** *truth*. In other words, *truth* is the unveiling, revealing, uncovering, and disclosing of that which is THE ULTIMATE REALITY! At the risk of being slightly repetitive, let's take just another moment to *drive this point home* to where it sinks down deep into the soul. When Jesus stated His mission was to bear witness unto the *truth*, He was conveying to all those who were and are able to perceive His words, that He was, is, and is to come as the Ultimate Reality, making known to all His actuality, His existence, His authenticity, and His presence as the Word (God) made flesh Who dwelled among us. Once again, He came to reveal, unveil, make public, broadcast, display, exhibit, publish, uncover, and show the world Who He was, and what He had come to accomplish, taking away the sin of the world! In order to further clarify the subject of *truth*, let us look to the Bible, for there are direct statements within its pages that clearly and precisely define *truth*. Before we do this, though, let us embrace the following words from Dr. Harold Lovelace. They will be most helpful in setting the stage for the rest of our quest for *truth*.

According to Dr. Harold Lovelace:

"Many people are satisfied with the status quo. They just accept what has been told to them for the *truth* and never question it. The *Truth* is so important, and it is the *Truth* that will make us free. **If we receive less than the full amount of *truth*, we are denying ourselves of God's blessings.** Everything you hold to be true should be tested, doubted, searched, and researched again against all reasonable standards to see if it is in fact the *Truth*." -end quote- (Read And Search God's Plan, Dr. Harold Lovelace)

TRUTH DEFINED BY THE SCRIPTURES

Who is it among us that does not want to be *made free*? If this is the case, then we should all the more seek to embrace and understand the words of Jesus, when He said, "*If* you continue in My word, then are you My disciples indeed; and **you shall know the *truth*, and the *truth* shall make you free**." (John 8:31-32) One of the most beautiful aspects of The Holy Scriptures is how they define for us the words which are used within its pages. Any topic or word found within the Scriptures will ultimately, somewhere within the Scriptures, be defined by a direct statement which explains the word in question. In rare instances where this is not the case, the word in question will be used in a way which clearly gives its meaning. (This means that the way a word is used determines its meaning.) With all of this being said, we can now put on our "Berean Cap" and search the Scriptures for the exact definition of *truth*.

According to The Holy Scriptures:

- **THE LAW IS THE *TRUTH* (Psalm 119:142)**
- **THE COMMANDMENTS ARE *TRUTH* (Psalm 119:151)**
- **ALL GOD'S WORKS ARE *TRUTH* (Daniel 4:37)**
- **JESUS IS THE *TRUTH* (John 14:6)**
- **THE WORD IS THE *TRUTH* (John 17:17)**
- **THE ANOINTING IS *TRUTH* (1st John 2:27)**
- **THE SPIRIT IS *TRUTH* (1st John 5:6)**

LAW / COMMANDMENTS / WORKS / JESUS / WORD / ANOINTING / SPIRIT

How exciting it is to have the exact definition of *truth* taken from seven direct statements out of the Scriptures! Putting all of this together, we have now discovered the precise meaning of *truth* (unveiled reality), and the avenues through which it is manifested, unveiled, and revealed to the world. This also tells us that The Law, The Commandments, God's Works, Jesus, The Word, The Anointing, and The Spirit are <u>all one in the same</u>. They are all *conduits* or *channels* (if you will) through which THE ULTIMATE REALITY, **WHICH IS GOD**, is distributed and made known to all people and all things. It would then be proper to say that all seven avenues mentioned in Scripture which distribute *truth* are the same as God, and that God is the same as all seven definitions of *truth*. For example, The Law, The Commandments, God's Works, Jesus, God's Word, The Anointing, and The Spirit are all the same as or equal to God, and the reverse of this is true also, in that God is the same as or equal to all seven things mentioned. Taking any one of the seven items we mentioned, we could say: The Law is God, and God is The Law…or… Jesus is God, and God is Jesus…and so on.

You obviously get the point by now. The very fact that all seven statements in Scripture define *truth* tells us that all seven are one in the same, for there can only be <u>one *truth*</u>, **WHICH IS GOD**. Having seven statements, though, using seven different terms, tells us that God manifests Himself (His *truth*) in at least these seven different ways to confirm and distribute His *truth* to the human race. We will not attempt at this time to write specifically concerning all seven statements pertaining to *truth*, for this would require a complete book in and of itself, but let it suffice for now to know of these seven statements; and may we pour our soul into each one in an effort to discover its full significance, meaning, value, and unique message as it pertains to *truth*. As we come to the conclusion of this teaching on the great topic of *truth*, there is one more point I wish to address and bring to your attention, and as they say…"*bring it on home*". I want us to focus again on the words of Dr. Harold Lovelace, when he stated, **"If we receive less than <u>the full amount of *truth*</u>, we are denying ourselves of God's blessings."** Let us be diligent and obedient students of the Word of God in order that we would truly receive all of God's blessings!

THE <u>FULL</u> <u>AMOUNT</u> OF *TRUTH*

Jesus is THE *TRUTH*! This is what we are told in John 14:6. If we were to take this statement and couple it with the statement made by Dr. Harold Lovelace concerning "the full amount of *truth*", then we would be left with this statement: If we receive less than "the full amount of JESUS CHRIST", we are denying ourselves of God's blessings. When I say…"the full amount of Jesus Christ", I am referring to the full understanding of Who He is and what He has accomplished through the blood of His cross. Too many Christians have settled for just a "vaccine" of the Lord Jesus Christ. They receive just enough of a weakened and watered-down version of Jesus Christ to actually make them **immune,** so that their "spiritual immune system" recognizes the true message of Jesus Christ as foreign and destroys it.

According to Wikipedia, The Free Encyclopedia:

"A **vaccine** is a biological preparation that improves immunity to a particular disease. A vaccine typically contains an agent that resembles a disease-causing microorganism, and is often made from weakened or killed forms of the microbe or its toxins. The agent stimulates the body's <u>immune system</u> to recognize the agent as foreign, destroy it, and "remember" it, so that the immune system can more easily recognize and destroy any of these microorganisms that it later encounters." -end quote- (<u>Vaccine</u>, Wikipedia, The Free Encyclopedia)

While many are told to believe on the Lord Jesus Christ for the justification of their spirit, very few are told to submit to God in and through the process of sanctification in order that their soul would be conformed into the image of God. As well, very few are taught the importance of understanding the glorification of the body at the time of resurrection, and that there shall be a "first resurrection" for the overcomers (leaders) in God's Kingdom. This is an example of "not receiving the full amount of the *truth*". Also, many are told that only a few -- The Barley Harvest -- will come to know the Lord in this present age, but there is hardly any teaching on the reconciliation of all things (The Church In General / The Wheat Harvest **&** The Unbelievers / The Grape Harvest) through the blood of the cross of Christ, and how this will play out through the "manifestation of the sons of God" in the ages to come. Here is another prime example of "not receiving the full amount of Jesus Christ".

In all of these cases it is as though a "vaccine" of Jesus Christ has been given, but not "the full amount", which is able to totally deliver, make free, and heal the soul of man from his inherited sin nature. Not receiving "the full amount of Jesus Christ" is the same as not fully understanding the **person** (Who He is) and **work** (what He has accomplished) of Jesus Christ. There are so many passages of Scripture when understood which declare the **person** and **work** of Christ, but one that is especially descriptive is Colossians 1:14-20. In this passage we are told of **Christ, Who is the image of the invisible God**, and that He created **all things**, and finally, that He has made peace through the blood of His cross to reconcile **all things** unto Himself! THIS IS THE FULL AMOUNT OF TRUTH! This is also why Paul spoke of "the whole counsel" of God. Once again, the longer we go in our walk with Christ and do not receive "the full amount of *truth*", the more susceptible we become to the "vaccine syndrome", in which we recognize the true message of Christ as foreign and destroy or abort it in our mind.

In this particular teaching we started out by asking the question…What Is *Truth*? In simple terms, Jesus is God and He is the Savior of **all**, every man in his own order! This is the explanation of the *truth*. The Law, The Commandments, God's Works, Jesus, The Word, The Anointing, and The Spirit all point to what we have just mentioned. I can think of no greater endeavor in this life than to aggressively pursue the knowledge of the *truth*, no matter what the cost may be. How fitting at this time to close this teaching with the dramatic and passionate words of the apostle Paul, when he stated…

But what things were gain to me, those I counted loss for Christ (The *Truth*). Yea doubtless, and I count all things but loss for the excellency of the knowledge of Christ Jesus my Lord: for whom I have suffered the loss of all things, and do count them but dung, that I may win Christ, and be found in Him, not having my own righteousness, which is of the law, but that which is through the faith of Christ, the righteousness which is of God by faith: that I may know Him, and the power of His resurrection, and the fellowship of His sufferings, being made conformable unto His death; if by any means I might attain unto the resurrection of the dead. Not as though I had already attained, either were already perfect: but I follow after, if that I may apprehend that for which also I am apprehended of Christ Jesus. Brethren, I count not myself to have apprehended: but this one thing I do, forgetting those things which are behind, and reaching forth unto those things which are before,

I press toward the mark for the prize of the high calling of God in Christ Jesus.

Philippians 3:7-14

PART 3 - BLIND FROM BIRTH

Have you ever considered that man is totally and completely blind to the things of God; so much so that he is also blind to the very existence of God until he has that great awakening accompanied with a born again experience through Jesus Christ? Well…of course you have considered these things if you are a Christian, but let us really stop and think about this for a moment. If we are as blind to the things of God as I have stated, then how is it that we find ourselves born into this peculiar conundrum so intricate and difficult a problem? Remember…Not only are we blind to the things of God, but we are *blind from birth*! Could it be that God is the author of our blindness? Did He predestine us to be born this way? Is He responsible for man being born into this condition? Some would say that it is all the fault of Adam and Eve, and that God never intended for man to be born blind to the knowledge of his Creator. If this were the case, though, it would support the idea that God does not have foreknowledge and sovereignty, which is not the case! God does have foreknowledge. God is sovereign. So…With all this being said, it is quite clear where our blindness came from. **It came from God!** Even though Adam's transgression was what brought sin into the world, this was but a vehicle designed and used by God to bring vanity and blindness upon all. If God wanted us to be born blind, then it must be for our good, and there are certainly specific reasons why this must be done to man. Are you shocked by these statements? Are you offended? Please do not be. Hang in there and let us turn to the Word of God for clear and direct statements which will not only support these claims, but which will also make us free to understand why God has made us *blind from birth*.

SUBJECT TO VANITY

Romans 8:20 tells us that "the creation was made subject to vanity, not willingly, but by reason of Him Who subjected the same in hope…" Here is this same verse as it reads from The New Testament In Modern Speech: "For the Creation fell into subjection to failure and unreality (not of its own choice, but by the will of Him Who so subjected it)."

We are also informed from the Scriptures that God created all things (Colossians 1:16), including the serpent / devil (Genesis 3:1 / Revelation 20: 2), darkness and evil (Isaiah 45:7), and all invisible powers of darkness for us to wrestle against (Colossians 1:16 / Ephesians 6:12). As well, we all know full well that we are born with an inherent sin nature passed down to us from Adam. Surely all of this should stop us in our tracks long enough for us to ponder the origin and purpose of our blindness. It is in and through the things just mentioned that God has afflicted the creation with vanity, failure, unreality, and *blindness from birth*. While many will try to argue against what has just been stated, these are direct statements from Scripture which prove that God is responsible for our blindness. For those who are mature enough in God to recognize and admit that God is responsible for lowering us into the soulish realm where we became subject to blindness, sin, and death, the question then becomes: What is the purpose and reason for our blindness?

THE WORKS OF GOD SHOULD BE MADE MANIFEST

If the truth be told, there are at least a few specific reasons that can and will be mentioned concerning our blindness by God from birth. First and foremost, though, we are given a clue as to our blindness from the Gospel of John, chapter nine, when it speaks of a man who was "blind from his birth". I do realize that this story was speaking of natural blindness, and that it was pertaining to one specific person, but for those of us who have "the spirit of wisdom and revelation" in the knowledge of Jesus Christ, we know that the Scriptures also have symbolic and hidden meaning in them waiting to be revealed to us by God. It is recorded that the disciples asked Jesus in John 9:2-3, saying, "Master, who did sin, this man, or his parents, that he was born blind?" Jesus answered, "Neither has this man sinned, nor his parents: **but that the works of God should be made manifest in him**." Jesus further explained Himself to the disciples in John 9:5, saying, "As long as I am in the world, I am the **light** of the world."

For those of you who are familiar with the rest of this story, you know how wonderful and beautiful it is. Jesus healed this man who was "blind from his birth". As usual, it caused an uproar among the Pharisees, for they claimed that Jesus was a sinner and not capable of such a miracle. The story ends with Jesus revealing Himself as the Son of God to the man He had just healed. But before this happens, the man who was healed gives one of the greatest one-liners of all time, when he says, "Whether He (Jesus) is a sinner, or not, I know not: **one thing I know, that, whereas I was blind, now I see**." (John 9:25) At the very end of the chapter Jesus rebukes the Pharisees because they refuse to admit their *spiritual blindness*, saying they can already see when they cannot. He tells them that if they do not repent and admit their blindness, then their sin (and blindness) will remain. As magnificent as this story is, it is not just Biblical history, but it is also an allegory which points to the fact that we are all *blind from birth*. Let's take a minute to explore the spiritual meaning of this story.

Obviously, the man in this story who was "blind from his birth" represents the human race, in that we have all been *born blind* to the knowledge of God and where we came from. The disciples, who were asking Jesus why this took place, who had sinned, and who was to blame for this occurrence, represent our lack of understanding concerning God's purpose. We do not understand it was God Who subjected us to vanity and blindness; and we continually blame man for the current condition of things instead of understanding and knowing that this present world is under the control of God and His purpose of the ages. The answer that Jesus gives to the disciples (Neither has this man sinned, nor his parents: **but that the works of God should be made manifest in him.**) is the *tell-all statement* which sheds the necessary *light* on the confusion as to why we are *blind from birth*. We are given a direct statement from the very lips of Jesus which clues us in as to the purpose of God and His dealings with the creation, in that **He desires to manifest Himself in and through us**, and has used *blindness from birth* as a means to accomplish this. This informs us beyond a shadow of a doubt that:

1. God is responsible for, and has caused our spiritual blindness.

2. God is pleased with our condition of being *blind from birth*, knowing that it will result in a greater good in the end, and He shall remove our blindness and give us all our sight back. But every man in his own order.

3. The works of God will be made manifest through our blindness.

Jesus then goes on to tell the disciples **He is the light of the world!** This is proof that He is the author and finisher of our blindness. If Jesus is **light**, and we find ourselves in **blindness**, then He has surely removed His **light** from us for a season and for a purpose, and has the power to remove our **blindness** and to restore us by "shining in our hearts the **light** of the glorious Gospel of Christ, Who is the image of God" (2nd Corinthians 4:4). Jesus' healing of the man in the story proves to us that He is light, and that He is capable of healing our blindness. The fact that Jesus spits on the *ground*, makes clay, anoints the eyes of the blind man, and tells him to wash in the Pool of Siloam, which causes him to receive his sight, tells us that Jesus has power over the *ground*, from which man has been made and returns to at physical death, and also over our mortality. In the full scheme of things, Jesus is able to raise us up from the power of the grave (the *ground*) and to give us crystal clear visibility as though we are seeing with the very eyes of God.

The other remaining elements in the story (the anger / unbelief of the Pharisees and the revelation of Jesus as the Son of God) point to the two reactions to the light of Jesus Christ. As always, we can either come to the light or run from the light. Those who humble themselves and admit their blindness will be healed from both their sin and blindness, while those who refuse to repent will no doubt remain, for the time being, in their sin and blindness, not *seeing* that Jesus Christ is the Son of God. The apostle John said it best when he stated in John 3:19-21, "And this is the condemnation, that light is come into the world, and men loved darkness rather than light, because their deeds were evil. For every one that does evil hates the light, neither comes to the light, lest his deeds should be reproved. But he that does truth comes to the light, that his deeds may be made manifest, that they are wrought in God." Not only does our *blindness from birth* allow the works of God to be made manifest in and through us, but it also gives God an avenue to be glorified in all the earth.

IT IS THE GLORY OF GOD TO CONCEAL A THING

I remember when I was writing my first book and still trying to come up with a title for it. The title (or name) of something is very important to me, not only the way it sounds and looks, but also the meaning that is to be found within the words that are used. I *toyed around* with several titles, but I could tell they did not have the "it factor" and were not the ones I was looking for. When I am trying to come up with a name or title for something I am not always sure in which direction to go, but when I hear or see the right one I know it for sure. The right one will resonate within and have a certain "ring" or sound to it. The name for the book just seemed to come to me one night *out of the blue*. Not only did I love the way it sounded and flowed together, but I also loved the meaning, which seemed to fit the very purpose of the book to a T. The name which God gave me (The Glory Of God & The Honor Of Kings) for the book comes from Proverbs 25:2, which states…"It is *the glory of God* to conceal a thing: but *the honor of kings* is to search out a matter." The word "conceal" used in this passage simply means: to **hide**. Also, the words "search out" that are used in this same verse mean: to **seek**. Is it true that God has hidden Himself and the truth from the world by causing us to be *blind from birth*? Well…Yes. This verse of Scripture helps to shed even more light on why God has done this and what His great underlying purpose is.

Surely all who are reading this remember at one time or another playing the childhood game called **"hide-and-go-seek"**. Well…now we know *Who* was the first *One* to invent the game. It appears that God is the author of this game, but in actuality it is not a game to God. It is His very purpose of the ages. We all remember how to play **"hide-and-go-seek"**. **"Hide-and-seek"** or **"hide-and-go-seek"** is a variant of the game *tag*, in which a number of players **"conceal"** themselves in the environment, to be found by one or more **"seekers"**. In our case (as far as God and His creation are concerned), God has concealed Himself, in that He has caused us to be *blind from birth* and continually on the lookout and seeking for Him even when we are not aware (in the beginning of our search) what or Who we are actually seeking for. According to Proverbs 25:2, THE GLORY OF GOD is to conceal a thing! Once again, God has concealed and hidden Himself from us by causing us to forget where we came from. He does this each time someone is born. It is the story of *Adam* and *Eve* played out all over again through the birth of every individual who has ever been born.

We are all born of the dust of the ground (with a body), with the breath of life (our spirit, which comes from God), and we become a living soul (having a mind, will, and emotions). Spiritually speaking, God causes a "deep sleep" to come upon us (*Adam* / our spirit). He then takes one of our ribs and makes a woman (*Eve* / our soul). We must understand that we all have *Adam* and *Eve* within us, which equates to our spirit and soul. Our spirit represents the masculine part of us and our soul represents the female part of us. When God does this, though, He separates the soul from the spirit. This causes us to be born into a condition where it is impossible to do anything else but to listen to and be deceived by the *serpent* (the spirit which works in the children of disobedience), which in turn causes us to automatically partake of *the tree of the knowledge of good and evil* (the carnal mind). As a result of this we are separated from God in our mind at birth until the time we believe on Him through His Son. God has also placed *the tree of life* (Christ in us the hope of glory) within us (our *Garden of Eden*), but it is impossible for us to see or know this until our spirit (*Adam*) comes out of the "deep sleep" that God has put us in.

Once the spirit of man is awakened to God through believing on the Lord Jesus Christ, which is justification by faith, it is then the task of God to make the spirit and soul one. This is where the sanctification of the soul takes place, and where the soul is…"transformed by the renewing of the mind, that we may prove what is that good, and acceptable, and perfect will of God." Paul spoke of this in Romans 12:1-2. Now we are able to understand the spiritual significance of Genesis 2:23-24, which states…"And Adam said, This is now bone of my bones, and flesh of my flesh: she shall be called Woman, because she was taken out of Man. Therefore shall a man leave his father and his mother, and shall cleave unto his wife: and they shall be one flesh." Not only do these verses pertain to a man and a woman, but they also represent the relationship between the spirit and the soul, and how the soul is to be married to the spirit in obedience to God. It is absolutely ***amazing*** to discover to what extent God has gone to in an effort to conceal Himself from us in order that He may have the pleasure of revealing Himself to us. He delights in the fact that we are *blind from birth*; because He knows we will forsake this temporal realm to chase hard after Him and to search out the matter.

Do you see yourself as a king searching out the matter of God under the Headship of The King of kings? God is a secret. He is hidden. **To really know Him is to go on a spiritual scavenger hunt**. Seek the Lord with all your heart and you will find Him. Remember…the honor of kings is to search out the matter. There is one last element of our *blindness* that we must explore before we bring this topic to a conclusion. It deals with the relationship of a master to his servant, and how **the law of God is actually designed to show mercy to all in the end**.

FREE FOR HIS EYE'S SAKE

Except we understand the purpose of the law of God, the Old Testament will remain useless to us and quite boring to say the least. Had it not been for a key statement made by Jesus to certain disciples after His resurrection, I would not cherish the law of God and the Old Testament to the degree I do now. In Luke chapter twenty-four (toward the end of the chapter) we are given specific information as to how Jesus reveals Himself to His disciples (and all for that matter). After speaking to two men on the road to Emmaus as well as His other disciples, on both occasions Jesus expounded unto them concerning Himself by taking them back to THE LAW OF MOSES, THE PROPHETS, and THE PSALMS. **It was only after this that their eyes were opened and they knew Him**. Jesus used THE LAW OF MOSES, THE PROPHETS, and THE PSALMS **to open their understanding, that they might understand the Scriptures**. While it may seem easier at first to understand God through the New Testament, you will never get the full revelation of Jesus Christ until you go back and look for Him in THE LAW OF MOSES, THE PROPHETS, and THE PSALMS. There you will *see* Him and your understanding will be opened up to understand the Scriptures in their totality. Seeing Jesus in this way will also magnify how you see Him in the New Testament, **for the New Testament is merely the manifestation and revelation of the *symbolism* of the Old Testament brought to light in the person and work of the Lord Jesus Christ**. With all this in mind, let us go back to the LAW OF MOSES in order to properly understand Jesus Christ as our Master in relationship to us as His servants who are *blind from birth*.

Exodus 21:26 (New Living Translation) states…"If a man hits his male or female slave in the eye and the eye is blinded, he must let the slave go free to compensate for the eye." The King James Version uses the terminology…"he shall let him go free for his eye's sake." Once the spiritual significance of this verse is realized it will make you free to where you would climb to the highest mountain and shout the truth of the matter for the entire world to hear and understand. Not only was this a law that applied to natural matters, but it also speaks of our *blindness from birth*. In this short verse we are told who the Author of our blindness is and the purpose for this condition. It is God Who has temporarily injured our spiritual eyes by subjecting us to vanity, including mortality, sin, and death. Here is the kicker, though: **This same God is now responsible and obligated by His own law to let ALL go free in the end for our eye's sake**. In other words, because God has *blinded all from birth* He *must* (according to His own law) bring ALL to a place of freedom, salvation, reconciliation, and restoration in the dispensation of the fullness of times. He must gather together in one ALL THINGS IN CHRIST (Ephesians 1:10)!

BUILT-IN PROTECTION / MERCY

How amazing is our God that He has actually designed for His creation built-in protection into His law to guarantee our salvation through Jesus Christ. The purpose of our *blindness from birth* in the grand scheme of things is to **protect us** and to assure the eventual regaining of our sight in God. For God to go to this extent, causing blindness and then giving us our sight again, shows several things about His character and nature. It proves that He is truly a God of **knowledge, wisdom, and design**. As well, it proves **His Great Love** for His creation, in that

He is willing to be patient with us as we go through this process for the purpose of correction, learning, and being made into His image. Finally, it showcases **God's grace and mercy** and proves that there is no limit to the depths of His love, grace, and mercy! Did you *hear* what was just said? THERE IS NO LIMIT TO THE DEPTHS OF GOD'S LOVE, GRACE, AND MERCY! Not only will our *blindness from birth* (which was caused by God) serve as instruction for us, causing us to mature into the likeness of our Heavenly Father, but it becomes a *trophy case* in which God shall display His mercy for all to see.

The word "mercy" means: kindness or good will towards the miserable and the afflicted, joined with a desire to help them. We are told in Romans 11:32 that…"God has concluded ALL in unbelief, that He might have *mercy* upon ALL." Is this not true? Haven't we all been born in affliction, sin, unbelief, vanity, futility, failure, frustration, and blindness? Well… Is it not true then also that God will have mercy on all? The answer to that is YES! **And thank God it is!** It matters not that most of those who call themselves Christians have no mercy in their heart for a world of unbelievers who will die lost. It will not stop God from waking the unbelievers up in the second resurrection and purifying them in and through the lake of fire for the purpose of correction and restoration in order to give them their sight back and to let them go free. No indeed… it will not stop God, WHO IS LOVE, in the slightest bit from extending His mercy to all. Not only does God want to show mercy to all and give sight to those who are blind, but He **must** let us all go free in the end for our eye's sake. It is His law, and He cannot go against His own law. Do not think for one minute that God wants to go against His own law, for that is absurd. He built "the mercy factor" into His law by design. Yes…He is a God of judgment, but His end goal (according to James 5:11) is to be…"very pitiful, and of tender mercy." This means that above all **God is full of pity, and that He is extremely compassionate**. His mercy will triumph over His judgment in the end. This is especially true because the very purpose of His judgment is to teach righteousness and to bring about correction. There is no vindictiveness in God, only correction!

Despite what most teach about God, He is kind and wants to show good will toward all. He is a God of help in our time of trouble. Once again, HE IS FULL OF PITY, AND HE IS EXTREMELY COMPASSIONATE! Believe it or not, we will actually thank God in the end for having been subjected to *blindness from birth*. Could we ever truly appreciate our sight in God had it not been for the *blindness* we have been afflicted with? God makes use of opposites to teach His creation, such as evil and good, hate and love, and blindness and sight. It is the only way for us to truly appreciate our salvation and for us to *see* how glorious our God is. Remember…"God has concluded ALL in unbelief, that He might have *mercy* upon ALL."

Here are the words from two of the most cherished songs of all time that do so adequately conclude this teaching…

Amazing Grace, how sweet the sound, That saved a wretch like me. I once was lost but now am found, <u>Was</u> <u>blind</u>, <u>but</u> <u>now</u> <u>I</u> <u>see</u>.

Mercy came running,

Like a prisoner set free.

Past all my failures to the point of my need,

When the sin that I carried,

Was all I could see.

And when I could not reach mercy,

<u>**Mercy**</u> <u>**came**</u> <u>**running**</u> <u>**to**</u> <u>**me.**</u>

PART 4 - LEARNING OBEDIENCE

It has been said (by Hosea Ballou) that…"Obedience sums up our entire duty." With this being said, it causes one to wonder why there is so little teaching, emphasis, and understanding on this subject. When most Christians hear the words "obedience", "law", "sanctification", "qualification", and "suffering", they act as though they have been put in a closed-in room with a rattle snake, looking for a way of escape. As well, the Bible is full of *conditional statements*, using terminology like: "**If** you do this, **then** this will (or will not) happen"…or…"**If** you do not do this, **then** this will (or will not) happen." They are conditional statements from God that require obedience that will result in a positive or negative consequence. We must be diligent students of the Word of God in order to rightly divide the subject matter of the Book. The idea of obedience is all through the Bible and does not clash with the idea of grace or justification by faith. Obedience, which is a learned behavior taught to us in and through our sanctification process, is actually an extension of grace and justification by faith. This is the whole purpose of the grace of God and our faith in Him. Are we not called to obey our God and become like Him in character and nature? Is not obedience the proof that we have embraced the grace of God and do believe in Him? Did not Jesus say…"If you love Me, you will obey what I command?" (John 14:15 / New International Version) And did not the apostle James say, "Faith without works is dead?" (James 2:20)

Unless we learn obedience and submit ourselves to the dealings of God, in which He shall transform our soul (mind, will, and emotions) into the likeness of His character and nature, then we fall short of our complete salvation, which includes spirit, soul, and body. To experience justification by faith only, not going on to learn obedience to our Master, is like baking a cake and not putting the icing on top. The best part is left out. Justification grants us "imputed righteousness", but obedience through sanctification causes us to literally "become righteous". You see…it is needful for us to be obedient in order for us to become what we have been declared to be. This is still a work of the Spirit, and not something we are able to accomplish in our own ability, but nevertheless, it must be recognized by us and submitted to in order for us to press into the high calling. Remember…**God is responsible** to do in us (by His Spirit) what we cannot do in and of ourselves, but **we are accountable** to recognize what is taking place and to submit (willingly) to our Lord's training. *Even the Son of God had to learn obedience by the things which He suffered!* This statement alone should drive us to understand the need for, importance, and purpose of obedience.

THOUGH HE WERE A SON

Hebrews 5:8 tells us…"Though He (Jesus) were a Son, yet learned He obedience by the things which He suffered." The word "Son" in this verse comes from the Greek word "huios" and is typically used and reserved for the Son of God and / or those who have matured into the likeness of the Son. "Huios" primarily signifies the relation of offspring to parent and not simply the birth as indicated by the Greek word "teknon". "Teknon" refers to those who were born of God (a child) and "huios" refers to those who show maturity acting as sons. When just the basic relationship as a born-again child of God is referred to, it is expressed as "teknon" (Romans 8:16). "Huios", though, gives evidence of the dignity of one's relationship and likeness to God's character (Romans 8:19). In John 1:12 "teknon" is used of new believers, not "huios". The expression "Son of God" ("huios Theou") is used of Jesus as a manifestation of His relationship with the Father or the expression of His character. The Lord Jesus is never called "teknon Theou", a child of God, as believers are. **(Commentary on "huios" and "teknon" from: <u>Lexical Aids To The New Testament</u>, Spiros Zodhiates)**

Having said all this, if Jesus (being a "huios" / the mature Son of God) was the express image of the Father in His role as the Son (though He were a Son), yet He still had to learn obedience by the things which He suffered, then where does that leave us? Surely if Jesus (the Son / "huios") had to go through this experience, then we must also learn obedience in the same way as a child ("teknon") of God. This principle proves to us that not only was Jesus a Son and a Savior, but He was also a Pattern. As a matter of fact, Bill Britton (in his writings) often referred to Jesus as *The Pattern Son*. Hebrews 2:9 tells us…"But we see Jesus, Who was made a little lower than the ***angels* (Elohim / God: see Psalm 8:5 and reference the word *angels* to its Hebrew origin)** for the suffering of death, crowned with glory and honor; that He by the grace of God should taste death for every man." In the next verse we are told that the goal of Jesus was and is to "bring many sons unto glory", and that…"the Captain of salvation was made perfect through sufferings." Well…what we have here is a pattern put in place by Jesus Himself, in which He and all who will become like Him must go through. It is one in which we must learn obedience by the things which we suffer.

LEARNING

Once again, the very fact that Jesus (as our Pattern) had to *learn* informs us of where we stand with God and where we are headed on this great journey of becoming like the Captain of our salvation. In simple terms, if Jesus had to learn, then so do we. The word "learn" in this verse speaks of: experience, bringing into experience, understanding, knowing, to know more fully, and to learn by use and practice accompanied with being accustomed to something or being in the habit of doing something. There are two examples which come to mind that will make this point extremely easy to understand and also show the need for learning and practice in the Kingdom of God. One example has to do with *children going to school* and the other has to do with *sports*.

There comes a day in the life of every child when it is necessary for him to be cut loose from mom's apron strings and to get out into the world on his own. This takes place when a child starts school for the first time. The parents are usually scared, upset, and sad that their child is off to school and no longer their little baby any more. It is a new experience for the child and the parents. Nevertheless, we all know that this experience is necessary in order to subject the child to an atmosphere where he can LEARN. The child must learn, experience, understand, and gain knowledge through practice and repetition. It is only in and through the atmosphere of school that the young student can become accustomed to and in the habit of being tested for the purpose of acquiring the needed skills to mature and blossom into an adult and a functioning member of society.

In addition to this illustration, those who participate in sports offer us another example as to the need for practice, repetition, and learning. Any person who has ever participated in organized sports knows the importance of practice. Young athletes are usually able to make it on talent alone, but the older one gets and the more he participates in sports, he will run into athletes who all have the same amount of talent or more. What separates the good athletes from the great athletes? Well…you guessed it. It is practice! When an athlete devotes himself to practice he is LEARNING discipline, work ethic, and the fundamentals of his individual sport. The practice experience develops and builds character while preparing the athlete for a real game-time situation. It is a simulation of the real thing…so that when he finds himself in the heat of the battle in an actual game he is prepared and ready to handle the challenge. What coach would subject his or her players into a game-time situation without having first brought them through repetitious practice and the proper drills to ensure they were battle tested and conditioned for the task at hand? I think we know the answer to that…none! School and sports offer us a clear and concise representation of the need for learning, practice, and repetition, in order to develop successful habits that lead us to victory in life.

When speaking of children and their need to learn in school and athletes being committed to practice, you will rarely come up against any type of opposition concerning these necessary experiences. On the other hand, though, when you speak of believers in Christ who are still in need of learning, practice, training, and qualification in the Kingdom of God, you will almost always find yourself in a *hornet's nest* of opposition, contrariness, and religious resistance. It is the strangest thing that we as humans recognize the need for learning in all aspects of life in order to grow, mature, and become qualified, but when it comes to God there seems to be a **disconnect** in this area. Most Christians, after going to church for a couple of months, and reading their Bible through one time, feel they are experts in a very short time. It is rare to come across a believer with a *teachable spirit* who has ears to hear coupled with an eagerness to learn and the spirit of humility. Most of this has to do with the leadership in the Kingdom of God and their lack of knowledge concerning the idea of sanctification as it pertains to the soul of the newly justified believer. For the most part, we are taught by Christian leaders that once we have been justified by faith in Jesus Christ that there is nothing left to our experience in God other than to *die and go to heaven*. As wonderful as it is that we have been justified, this is but an introduction that should bring us to the next phase of our salvation, whereby we are now able to learn obedience to God, not only as our Savior, but also as our LORD!

OBEDIENCE

As was stated in the beginning of this teaching, it is a shame that (for the most part) words like "obedience", "law", "sanctification", "qualification", and "suffering", are treated as *dirty words* in Christian circles. It all stems from a lack of teaching and understanding of how God is qualifying us as leaders in His Kingdom. It is important at this time to note that **this is a work of the Spirit of God**, and we are not referring to legalism, the flesh, or self-effort. There is a way to obey God in the Spirit and have His law (His Word / His character and nature) written on the heart and not go into legalism and self-righteousness. Take for example what was mentioned in Jeremiah 31:31, when it states…

Jeremiah 31:31-33 (King James Version)

³¹Behold, the days come, says the LORD, that I will make a new covenant with the house of Israel, and with the house of Judah:

³²Not according to the covenant that I made with their fathers in the day that I took them by the hand to bring them out of the land of Egypt; which My covenant they broke, although I was an Husband unto them, says the LORD:

³³But this shall be the covenant that I will make with the house of Israel; After those days, says the LORD, <u>I will put My law in their inward parts, and write it in their hearts</u>; and will be their God, and they shall be My people.

Can we not see the simplicity of the explanation of the two covenants of God? The goal of God has always been the same down through history in both of the covenants mentioned. It is this: That man would be made into the image of God, and that he would possess internally the law (character and nature) of God, enabling him to (by nature) be of the same essence as God Himself. The first covenant featured man's ability to accomplish this task. The second covenant features God's ability. It is just that simple! We all know that when man was given the opportunity to keep the law of God in his own ability, he failed miserably. This is evident from reading the Old Testament. But we also know that Jesus came, and that He fulfilled the law on our behalf, for He stated in Matthew 5:17-20…"Think not that I am come to destroy the law, or the prophets: **I am not come to destroy, but to fulfill**. For verily I say unto you, till heaven and earth pass, one jot or one tittle shall in no wise pass from the law, till all be fulfilled. Whosoever therefore shall break one of these least commandments, and shall teach men so, he shall be called the least in the kingdom of heaven: but whosoever shall do and teach them, the same shall be called great in the kingdom of heaven. For I say unto you, that except your righteousness shall exceed the righteousness of the scribes and Pharisees, you shall in no case enter into the kingdom of heaven."

Once we are able to see that not only are we called to believe on the Lord Jesus, but that we are also called to become like Him in character and nature, then we are able to comprehend the value of learning obedience, and how this factors into the sanctification of our soul. It is important to note, however, that we are not speaking of a legalistic effort (emphasizing the letter of the law over the spirit of the law) on our part. Learning obedience speaks more so of learning **submission** to the Spirit of God as He puts His law in our inward parts, and writes it in our hearts. Even though this is a work of the Spirit, God, through His infinite knowledge and wisdom, still incorporates and factors our limited will and ability to choose into the equation. While I do not side with those who teach we have a so-called "free will" (the ability to make *uncaused* choices), I do believe that we are able to make choices under the umbrella of God's sovereignty as He allows us to do so. This is brought out in the Bible in the form of accountability, stewardship, and what we do with the amount of authority God gives to us.

The word "obedience" carries with it the meaning of *willing subjection* to that which, in the sphere of divine revelation, is right. It is *willing subjection* to the saving will of God revealed in Christ. If it is true then (as stated by Hosea Ballou) that "Obedience sums up our entire duty", then we must ever seek to be in this frame of mind. It is the mindset that first <u>recognizes</u>, then <u>believes</u>, and finally <u>submits</u>. Once it is brought to our attention that we are not able to put God's law in our inward parts, and that we are not able to write it in our hearts through self-effort, we are then immediately ushered into the presence of God, looking to Him through Christ for the answer and deliverance of our soul. You see…it is the soulish part of man (his mind, will, and emotions) that must submit and become united (in marriage) to the Spirit of Christ in us the hope of glory. This is the part of our being that is called to learn obedience. And this is the process whereby our soul should "not be conformed to this world: but be transformed (go through a metamorphosis) by the renewing of our mind, that we may prove what is that good, and acceptable, and perfect will of God." (Romans 12:2)

To be ignorant or in denial of this necessary transformation, which goes hand in hand with learning obedience, is to be ignorant or in denial of our personal salvation. There are so many dear Christians who either know nothing of what is being presented here, or they have been led astray by seducing spirits and doctrines of demons into thinking they are exempt from being trained by God in this area. Remember…we asked the question earlier in this teaching, what coach or employer would place a person in a position of leadership who was unqualified and without proper training? For those who read this and are unaware of the call to sanctification, please apply yourself to understand the need to learn obedience.For those who read this and are in denial that salvation is a process (spirit, soul, and body), please consider your ways and re-evaluate your beliefs by putting them to the test in and through the Scriptures. Since it has been mentioned that we are in no way capable of performing this task through self-effort, it would only be right at this time to at least briefly mention the *power source* through which we gain the ability to go through our transformation into the image of God.

SUBMISSION TO THE SOURCE / THE DIVINE NATURE

In order to be a leader in God's Kingdom we must go from a child of God to a fully mature son (or daughter) of God. We must also learn obedience through the things we suffer. This is the pattern set forth by Jesus, The Pattern Son of God. If we set out on this journey (after having placed our faith in the sacrifice of Jesus Christ, being justified by faith), in our own strength, then we are destined to stumble and fall. Self-effort alone will surely lead to self-righteousness, pride, and ruin. If the goal is to become like God, then we must *get ahold of the stuff* that God is made of. We are all witnesses (through the Scriptures) how that man (in his own ability), when presented with the initial covenant of God, was only able to miserably fail and break God's covenant. However, we have now been made aware of the New Covenant of God through the death, burial, and resurrection of Jesus Christ on our behalf. We are all witnesses of the power of justifying faith in our Savior and have been *imputed* His righteousness through that faith. The apostle Peter, though, did not stop at faith alone when describing our experience in God. Here is what he said in 2nd Peter 1:5-11…

2nd Peter 1:5-11 (King James Version)

⁵And beside this, giving all diligence, ADD TO YOUR FAITH virtue; and to virtue knowledge;

⁶And to knowledge temperance; and to temperance patience; and to patience godliness;

⁷And to godliness brotherly kindness; and to brotherly kindness charity.

⁸For if these things be in you, and abound, they make you that you shall neither be barren nor unfruitful in the knowledge of our Lord Jesus Christ.

⁹But he that lacks these things is blind, and cannot see afar off, and has forgotten that he was purged from his old sins.

¹⁰Wherefore the rather, brethren, give diligence to make your calling and election sure: for if you do _(continually produce or repeat)_ these things, you shall never fall:

¹¹For so an entrance shall be ministered unto you abundantly into the everlasting kingdom of our Lord and Savior Jesus Christ.

The question to be associated with all of this is (as the apostle Paul asked in Romans 7:18): How to perform that which is good? How do we "do" (continually produce or repeat) these things? At first glance it would seem that God is asking us to muster up enough internal strength and fortitude to "do" these things on our own. But we know that this cannot be the case, for we have already seen the result of what happens when man goes down that road. It must be that the "doing" of this godly behavior is a *result* of having received divine power from the divine nature of our Heavenly Father. Oh my…yes…this is the answer! We have struck oil! We have found the answer to the question of the ages pertaining to deliverance from our sin nature. "Partaking" produces "doing"! Is this not what James said? *Ahhh*…it is all beginning to make sense now. Yes…faith without works is dead. Well…how do we continually produce the works of God? Believe it or not, this all has to do with learning obedience (submission). Let's take just another moment to stop and have a cup of coffee with the apostle Peter as he gives us the answer. Once again, here is what Peter had to say about the matter…

2nd Peter 1:3-4 (King James Version)

³According as His divine power has given unto us all things that pertain unto life and godliness, through the knowledge of Him that has called us to glory and virtue:

⁴Whereby are given unto us exceeding great and precious promises: that by these you might be partakers of the divine nature, having escaped the corruption that is in the world through lust.

Here is where obedience comes into the picture. It is not our job to change ourselves into the image of God, for that is impossible. God does require, though, that we recognize His divine power as the power source which is able to give us *all things* that pertain to life and godliness through the knowledge of Him. We are to *believe* these promises and to continually submit to the process of God, in which we become partakers of the divine nature. It is only through this that we will be able to escape the corruption and lust that is in the world. Once again, it is submission and obedience that God requires, through which He will "do these things" in and through us by His divine power, causing us to never fall. The end result is that we become one with God in nature. All of this speaks of the sanctification process, in which we find ourselves no longer acting out of self-effort, but acting out of the very nature of God. Finally, let us speak of the last concept in the original Scripture passage quoted (Hebrews 5:8) in the beginning of this teaching. The English word "suffered" was used to describe the process by which the Son of God learned obedience.

SUFFERING

According to Matthew Henry's Concise Commentary (Hebrews 5:1-10):

"Christ has left us an example that we should learn humble obedience to the will of God, by all our afflictions. We need affliction, to teach us submission. His obedience in our nature encourages our attempts to obey, and for us to expect support and comfort under all the temptations and sufferings to which we are exposed." -end quote- (Matthew Henry's Concise Commentary, Matthew Henry)

We are told from the Scriptures that Jesus learned obedience by the things He *suffered*. If He as the Son of God had to undergo sufferings, then we know we must also partake of this experience. The word "suffered" points to the fact that it is needful for all of the sons and daughters of God to be exposed to afflictions, trials, temptations, tests, and sometimes painful experiences (whether in the natural or the spiritual realm). It also refers to the idea of "feeling", "undergoing", and "enduring" certain life experiences and situations. It is vexation (irritation and annoyance) either caused or allowed by God for the purpose of bringing His children to a place of maturity in Him, and to where they will learn obedience. It is not that we want these things to happen or that we enjoy going through them, but we must face reality and acknowledge their presence and usefulness in bringing us to the end of our journey in God. WE MUST UNDERSTAND AND ACKNOWLEDGE THAT GOD IS THE AUTHOR OF SUFFERING AND AFFLICTION, BUT THAT IT IS FOR OUR GOOD, AND THAT IT WILL RESULT IN OUR LATTER END BEING MORE BLESSED THAN OUR BEGINNING!

Surely God is able to work all things together for our good! Surely He is able to deliver us from every affliction we face! The apostle Paul said (in Romans 5:3) that he gloried in his tribulations, because he knew what the outcome would be. He knew that his tribulations would result in patience, experience, hope, and love. This is just another way of saying that Paul learned obedience through the things he suffered, and that he was a partaker of the divine nature, for it is impossible to have patience, experience, hope, and love outside of the nature of God. Paul understood first and foremost that God was sovereign, and that his tribulations, trials, tests, temptations, and his thorn in the flesh were all designed and sent by God for a specific purpose and to bring about a specific outcome. He understood the process of sanctification and how God matured the believer into a fully mature son of God, knowing that if these elements of resistance were removed there would be no way to properly bring about the transformation of the soul into the image of God. Because Paul knew these things he was able to rejoice in the midst of suffering.

We can also be greatly encouraged and instructed from two key Scripture verses that are to be found in Psalm 34:19 and Psalm 119:71. They state…"Many are the afflictions of the righteous: but the LORD delivers him out of them all…&…It is good for me that I have been afflicted; that I might learn Your statutes." These verses tell us that suffering and affliction are part of the Christian journey, but that God will deliver us out of all our troubles, and that these afflictions are brought on to help us learn (obedience through the things we suffer). We are also told by Paul in 2nd Timothy 2:12 that…"If we suffer (endure), we shall also reign with Him…" And finally, Paul stated in Romans 8:18…"For I reckon that the sufferings of this present time are not worthy to be compared with the glory which shall be revealed in us."

My hope and prayer for all who read these words is that they will come alive to you by the spirit of wisdom and revelation that comes by the knowledge of Jesus Christ. This is our calling. This is the path for the sons and daughters of God who can hear the call to come up higher and to be an overcomer in the Kingdom of God. This is what it means to be elected for leadership as a king and priest unto God on behalf of the nations of this world. It comes with a price to pay and a cup to drink, but Paul said that the reward will be so much greater than the suffering. What little suffering we go through in this life, whether it is financial struggles, health problems, persecutions, or anything for that matter, will pale in comparison when we come forth as the fully victorious and triumphant manifested sons and daughters of God for all the world to see. Jesus Christ shall be fully manifested in the great cloud of witnesses as His overcomers display their glorified bodies as proof they have overcome death, hell, and the grave…AND EVERY EYE SHALL SEE HIM THROUGH US (Revelation 1:7), AND THE CREATION SHALL BE DELIVERED FROM THE BONDAGE OF CORRUPTION INTO THE GLORIOUS LIBERTY OF THE CHILDREN OF GOD (Romans 8:21). Even so, Amen!

PART 5 - HOW SAY SOME AMONG YOU THERE IS NO RESURRECTION OF THE DEAD?

This chapter includes excerpts from my discussion group on Yahoo (The Berean Group). The subject matter of this debate pertains to questions and challenges from one of the members of the group in reference to their belief that they will never physically die, and their belief that there is no such thing as a bodily resurrection of the dead. I have included several of my responses (along with one response from another member of the group) concerning this **extremely important topic**.

RESPONSE #1

The "never die" doctrine has been around for quite some time now. Unfortunately, it is a false doctrine. The only way to embrace this doctrine (teaching) is to completely deny and / or ignore the teaching of the apostle Paul concerning the resurrection (anastasis) of the dead. It stems from a spiritualizing of the term resurrection, which is an incorrect interpretation of the Scriptures. While it is true that we do have life NOW, having passed from death to life by believing on the Lord Jesus Christ (justification by faith), it is not true that we have been fully sanctified or glorified yet. We are presently waiting for these things to take place. In essence, our spirit has been awakened, but our soul is in the process of being saved, and our body is yet to be saved. As plain and simple as these things are, still yet, there are those who will not see the light concerning this teaching. Despite clear and direct statements from the Scriptures that teach otherwise, and the fact that there is no proof of *{any soul}* who has ever lived that did not go the way of the grave (including JESUS HIMSELF), some will still believe this teaching.

(...other than Enoch and Elijah - who, even though they did not go the way of the grave in the normal sense, are still not able to be seen, and are not in the visible realm: meaning they are still awaiting the resurrection of their bodies.)

It is not that one has to die (physically) to get "the life of the ages", for one does not. But God has designed a principle in His Kingdom that in order for life (as it pertains to the body) to come forth there must be a death first. A body cannot be resurrected unless it is dead. Jesus was and is the Pattern for all of this. If it was meant for us to never die, then surely Jesus would have walked out this pattern for us and He would still be alive in His same body and walking the earth today. Not only is this Scriptural, but it is common sense.

I have dealt with those who embrace the "never die" teaching for some time now. With the authority of the Holy Scriptures, I can say that it is incorrect. Once again, it all stems from a lack of understanding concerning spirit (justification), soul (sanctification), and body (glorification). It also stems from the blatant denial of what Paul taught concerning the resurrection of the dead.

Remember...Yes...we do have the life of God now (being seated with Him in heavenly places / raised with Him in newness of life now). This, however, does not speak of our sanctification and glorification. We MUST rightly divide the Scriptures concerning these topics. So many can only see one aspect of the Scriptures while completely ignoring other aspects.

It is not my intention to offend any concerning these comments. I am passionate, though, to guard against this particular teaching. If we remove the hope of resurrection and waiting as part of the Christian process, then we will (as Paul taught) destroy the faith of others.

Note: I do believe, however, that there will be a group of Christians who will be alive at the time of the first resurrection and who will put on immortality and not go the way of the grave in that sense. Paul did speak of this. He did not, however, speak of individuals beating death if they just happen to believe hard enough that they won't die. Also: Many use John 11:25-26 and John 8:51 in an improper way to support the "never die doctrine". It is actually speaking of not dying during the Messianic Age. It is not about receiving immortality per se, but about receiving immortality for the Messianic Age. Be sure to read these verses in the Concordant Literal Version.

RESPONSE #2

I will never disagree that there is a spiritual aspect to death and life that we have already entered into now. I really do not think that is where the problem of this discussion lies. We know we are born dead in sins and trespasses and that when we believe on the Lord Jesus Christ that we pass from death to life. This speaks of our justification by faith. In essence, our spirit has been raised at this point. The problem is that there is little or no teaching about the rest of the process of salvation.

Sanctification deals with the process of our soul being conformed into the image of God. It is not immediate, but it is gradual. Many refuse to accept this part of their salvation, claiming they are not waiting on anything, but that they are already a complete product. This is incorrect and the Scriptures bear this out. Paul told us that we have the "firstfruits" of the Spirit and that we are "waiting" for THE REDEMPTION OF OUR BODIES. Yes...those who have died are alive in the Spirit and on special occasions they are able to be manifested into the visible realm, but this is not the resurrection. The resurrection (anastasis) is an event that Paul spoke of clearly in 1st Corinthians chapter 15, for which he used the resurrection of Jesus as the example. The resurrection of Jesus was not a spiritual thing in His mind, but it was an actual event, whereby He stood on the earth again with a body that could no longer die and was not subject to the things His original flesh was subject to.

To deny the resurrection of the dead in general is to deny the resurrection of the Lord Jesus Himself. Paul made this very clear. All of the things in this argument being spoken of for the most part are referring to justification. And yes...we are already justified now. We are not waiting to be justified in a greater sense. We need to make sure, though, that we do not get out of balance and only quote one type of Scripture. There are plenty of Scriptures that also need to be quoted pertaining to our sanctification and the raising of our bodies.

RESPONSE #3

Matthew 6:9-10 (King James Version):

⁹After this manner therefore pray: Our Father which art in heaven, Hallowed be Thy name. ¹⁰Thy kingdom come, Thy will be done in earth, as it is in heaven.

The simplicity of the purpose of God is stated in these two short verses. In simple terms, we are told that God is a Spirit and that He dwells in the heavenly realm, but His purpose of the ages is to be manifested in the physical realm (in the earth). In order for Spirit to be manifested in the physical realm it is necessary for there to be a soul and a body. This is the whole reason why God subjected us to vanity, giving us a body and causing us to become a living soul. Because we are in vanity, though, we are subject to mortality at this time.

At the point we believe on the Lord Jesus Christ our spirit is awakened and the spark of the life of God comes into us. This, however, is the **firstfruits** of the Spirit, which then leads us through sanctification and prepares us for glorification. Paul told us...

Romans 8:22-25 (King James Version):

²²For we know that the whole creation groans and travails in pain together until now. ²³And not only they, but ourselves also, which have the firstfruits of the Spirit, even we ourselves groan within ourselves, waiting for the adoption, to wit, the redemption of our body. ²⁴For we are saved by hope: but hope that is seen is not hope: for what a man sees, why does he yet hope for? ²⁵But if we hope for that we see not, then do we with patience wait for it.

When a person physically dies they do "step into" the spirit realm and they are given a spirit body (2nd Corinthians 5:1-8), but this is still not "resurrection" as Paul spoke of in 1st Corinthians 15.

Here is what we must understand: We don't get the promise (of resurrection / our immortal body in the physical realm) by dying, or even by being present with the Lord in spirit form. We get our reward by getting the glorified body, which comes by resurrection. Spirit by itself is yet unrewarded, even if with God.

Those who submit to the sanctification of God will be those who qualify to be a part of the first resurrection. These are not just citizens in the Kingdom of God, but these are the leaders - the manifestation of the sons of God. How can the sons of God be MANIFESTED if they are not in the physical realm with a body? Once again, though, we are to understand that in order to manifest the fullness of God we will need to shed this mortality and put on immortality as Paul spoke of. In order to live through the Tabernacles Age and to teach the nations we will need for this corruption to put on incorruption. The end goal of the believer is not to go into the spirit (invisible) realm and stay there. It is to be manifested into the physical realm with a glorified body in which we will demonstrate the Kingdom of God in its highest form ON THE EARTH! Remember...Thy Kingdom come, Thy will be done in earth, as it is in heaven. Yes...the Kingdom of God is in us now, but remember we possess it in the form of the "firstfruits". At the time of resurrection we will possess it and demonstrate it in the earth in the fullness. Jesus is the Pattern for all of this, for this is the pattern He set for us. After His resurrection He said He had all power IN HEAVEN AND EARTH. This was because He now possessed an immortal body, giving Him the fullness in both realms.

Job so eloquently spoke of his hope in the resurrection when he explicitly stated that even after his mortal flesh was destroyed, there would still come a day when he would stand on the earth and see his Redeemer with his eyes. He was NO DOUBT speaking of the resurrection. Here is his statement...

Job 19:25-27 (King James Version):

[25]For I know that my redeemer lives, and that He shall stand at the latter day upon the earth: [26]And though after my skin worms destroy this body, yet in my flesh shall I see God: [27]Whom I shall see for myself, and mine eyes shall behold, and not another; though my reins be consumed within me.

WOW!!!

The conclusion of the matter is this: To deny the bodily resurrection of the dead in general is to deny the resurrection of Jesus Christ. Paul drove this point home for all to know for all of time that he believed in the bodily resurrection of the dead, and that He used the resurrection of Jesus as the pattern for the resurrection of the rest of the dead. There is no misunderstanding what he was saying. In first Corinthians 15 Paul was not spiritualizing the term (anastasis) resurrection when he spoke of the body. It is plain and simple to see what he was saying. It is whether or not we will accept this part of the purpose of God by faith or deny it as the Sadducees, Greeks, and Gnostics did. It is just that simple!

To deny the bodily resurrection of the dead is to deny Jesus Christ, Christianity, and our faith. This is a very important matter that must be looked into and rightly divided.

RESPONSE #4 (By Billy Thompson)

The resurrection then is the act of the Father by which He appoints Christ to be the Judge. He is raised not only for our justification who believe, but for the judgment of those who do not believe. The Father attested to Him as Savior, Son, and as Judge by His resurrection from the dead.

The real issue is not: Can you prove the resurrection? The real issue is: What does the resurrection prove? Take out the resurrection and it cuts out the soul of the Christian faith, left with non-Christianity. God's entire complete redemptive plan depends on this key reality.

And that brings it right down to us, doesn't it? Don't you know that the saints will judge the world? Don't you know that in order to reign with Him…you must suffer with Him? Don't you know that God will not leave your soul in Hades? Don't you know that God will grant you to become visible? Don't you know that if you die you shall be raised again? Don't you know that you shall inherit the heathen? Don't you know you shall inherit the earth? If the earth is invisible…what's the point?

Luke chapter 24 tells us of two woebegone, saddened and grieving disciples on the road to Emmaus who are walking along, thinking their Lord has perished for good, not knowing of His resurrection. They are sad, supposing all is lost. As Jesus comes alongside in verse 25 He says to them…"O foolish men and slow of heart, to believe in all that the prophets have spoken, was it not necessary for the Christ, the Messiah, to suffer these things and to enter into His glory? And beginning with

Moses and with all the prophets He explained to them the things concerning Himself in all the scriptures."

When the people see us in the Tabernacles Age they will rejoice and know that God has given them hope. They will see us in the fullness of the Spirit and not a mere earnest of the Spirit which we have received in this age. At the present...we are being preserved until that Day - "The Appointed Day" - that God has established, and not man. Yes... God's plan is to bring the invisible into the visible.

RESPONSE #5

Romans 8:22-25 (King James Version):

[22] For we know that the whole creation groans and travails in pain together until now. [23] And not only they, but ourselves also, which have the firstfruits of the Spirit, even we ourselves groan within ourselves, waiting for the adoption, to wit, the redemption of our body. [24] For we are saved by hope: but hope that is seen is not hope: for what a man sees, why does he yet hope for? [25] But if we hope for that we see not, then do we with patience WAIT for it.

If we have access to the "fullness" now, then what was Paul talking about and why was he waiting for something that had not happened yet?

Here is where the rubber meets the road. If there are those who say we can become immortal now and we do not have to wait, what are they waiting for to manifest this to us and the world? There is only proof in manifestation, and at this present time the only one to manifest immortality is Jesus Christ. He is the firstfruits of them that slept. And yes...we have been awakened from that sleep and given the earnest of the Spirit. But let us rightly divide the Word of truth. The earnest is not the fullness. As Paul said, there is an appointed time for our immortality and the redemption of our body.

RESPONSE #6

Remember to rightly divide the Word of truth. To make a general sweeping statement that we are not waiting on anything else in our experience with God is incorrect. We are definitely not waiting on the earnest of the Spirit of the life of God in us. We have that now. But we are waiting on:

-the completion of our sanctification process

-the redemption of our body

-the manifestation of the sons of God

These things have not happened yet. They are for an appointed time. God incorporates appointed times and waiting into His purpose and plan. We can either accept this, or try to achieve it on our own (which is really just self-effort clothed in religion).

Be careful not to turn your relationship with God into "you" trying to get immortality before the appointed time. First and foremost, it will not happen, but worse than that, you run the risk of frustrating the grace of God and continually walking in the flesh (trying to do something in your own ability which will not happen until the appointed time anyway).

You can deny the fact that we have been subjected to vanity and we are still subject to mortality in this age if you like, but it will not change the fact of the matter. The Tabernacles Age is set aside for immortality to be manifested through the sons of God.

If you study the Three Feasts of God (Passover, Pentecost, & Tabernacles), you will see that they beautifully paint a picture of all of this on the individual and corporate level.

On the individual level we are saved spirit, soul, and body. On the corporate level the creation will be saved: overcomers, the church in general, and the unbelievers. If you don't take the time to study the purpose and plan of God (beyond just you and your ability to try to get immortality now), you will not understand the ages and how they play a part in the purpose of God. We all want to get it "all" now. That is our plan. But God's plan has to do with appointed times. The earnest is available to us now, and the fullness will be available in the Tabernacles Age.

RESPONSE #7

The whole issue we are talking about here is whether or not God can or will raise up the body to a state of immortality in the visible physical realm. We know that God can and will do this because He did it with Jesus. So why would it be out of character for God to do it again with the rest of the creation? It is something He has already done.

The Greeks mocked the idea that the body could or would be raised. So also did the Sadducees and the Gnostics. Those who deny the bodily resurrection of the dead deny the resurrection of Jesus Christ, as did the three categories just mentioned.

Once again, Paul stated in 1st Corinthians 15 that to deny the resurrection of the dead in a bodily sense is to deny the resurrection of Jesus Christ.

Since you deny the bodily resurrection of the dead, are you o.k. with believing the same thing that the Greeks, Sadducees, and Gnostics did?

Acts 17:31-32 (King James Version):

[31]Because He has appointed a day, in the which He will judge the world in righteousness by that man Whom He has ordained; whereof He has given assurance unto all men, in that He has raised Him from the dead. [32]And when they heard of the resurrection of the dead, some mocked: and others said, we will hear thee again of this matter.

RESPONSE #8

John 8:51 (Concordant Literal Version):

[51]Verily, Verily, I am saying to you, if ever anyone should be keeping My word, he should under no circumstances be beholding death for the eon.

Once again (just like John 11:26), this is about receiving immortality for the Messianic Age. It is not about immortality per se, but about receiving immortality for the Messianic Age. It factors in the timing of one's resurrection, not merely the fact of immortality.

The Greek word for "never" in this verse is "aion".

It is a reference to the Age of Tabernacles in which the manifestation of the sons of God shall take place. Those who have kept the word of God during their time of sanctification (while being subjected to mortality by God) shall be those who will qualify to be the leaders in the Kingdom of God. They will be awarded with immortal bodies and no longer be subject to death during this age mentioned and beyond. But once again, this will be based off of those who submitted to sanctification, and that it is "the appointed time" of God for this to be manifested. It shall happen in a corporate sense. There is an appointed time for this to take place. **We are not able to make immortality happen simply by saying we will believe hard enough for it to happen when we want it to.**

PART 6 - GOD'S SOVEREIGNTY AND MAN'S AUTHORITY

It is far too often that I come in contact with Christians whose beliefs are out of balance, or they are overemphasized in one area or another of their understanding of God, while completely neglecting "the other side of the coin". One such example of this is the long-standing debate between *God's sovereignty* and *man's so-called free will*. An article of this nature has already been written by Dr. Stephen Jones (from which we will quote certain passages), but I wanted to *chime in* on this subject as well, for I am passionate about the topic at hand. The question at hand is really one of **balance**, more so than it is whether we understand all the elements of *God's sovereignty* and *man's will*. We will never fully grasp all the mysteries of *God's sovereignty* and how our *will* plays a part in the overall plan of God, BUT WE ARE CALLED UPON BY GOD TO RECOGNIZE BOTH ELEMENTS - SOVEREIGNTY & MAN'S WILL! My heart and passion for God's people is that they would understand the whole counsel of God and stop camping out on single elements of the Word of God and erecting their own kingdoms, ideas, and denominations in the name of God. This is nothing more than childishness, immaturity, and a refusal to take the time to grow up and rightly divide the Holy Scriptures. We must guard against becoming an extremist with unbalanced views, which keeps our growth and understanding of God stunted. It will be our goal in this teaching to show the balanced Scriptural view of *God's sovereignty* and *man's (God-given) authority*.

A BALANCED VIEW

The following words by Dr. Stephen Jones are most helpful, in that they expose the utter ridiculousness of holding an unbalanced view of *God's sovereignty* and *man's will*. They also show the pitfalls of clinging to a view that is skewed or distorted.

According to Dr. Stephen Jones:

"There is a long-standing debate between those who believe in *man's free will* and those who say that God's *sovereignty* disposes of *man's free will*. The "free will" side rightly emphasizes man's *responsibility* and *accountability* before God, yet often they tend to reduce God to the role of bystander or observer who is "ready to help" but in the end is really powerless against the *real* power - man.

On the other hand, the "sovereignty" side rightly emphasizes God's *sovereignty* and *power* over His creation, yet often they tend to use this to justify their sin by casting all *responsibility* upon God for their actions. Another way this can affect people is to paralyze them into doing nothing on the grounds that "God is doing it all".

Each side of the debate emphasizes different parts of Scripture, and each side has its truth. The problem is that many have too much truth on one side or the other of the issue, which makes their view unbalanced. The solution is to believe both that God is *sovereign* and that man has been given *authority* in the earth. These are not mutually exclusive ideas. To be "sovereign" does NOT mean that God is inherently all-powerful, but for some reason is not allowed to use that power in the earth without man's "free-will" consent. On the other hand, man's *authority* is NOT the same as "free will", although many have confused the two and have tried to prove "free will" by pointing to Scriptures that establish man's *authority*. Only *sovereignty* has *free will*. *Authority* is limited." -end quote- (How To Believe In God's Sovereignty Without Being A Fatalist, Dr. Stephen Jones)

Is it possible for God to be completely *sovereign* (to have supreme, indisputable, and independent authority and power) and for man to also possess a *will*? Well…sure it is, for this is what the Bible teaches. Just because God is *sovereign* does not necessarily mean that He forces and commands our every action and thought, even though He is able to do so. As well, just because we have a *will* does not mean that we are *totally free* to do whatever we want whenever we want. The *will of man* is actually a *limited will* and is ultimately subject to the *sovereignty* of God. There are plenty of Scriptures which declare the *sovereignty* of God, but there are also plenty of Scriptures which point to the fact that God requires us to make certain *choices*, and that He demands *responsibility, accountability, and stewardship*.

It is easy to take either of these two ideas and lean to one side of what seems to be a debate. There are major denominations today that are built off of just siding with the *sovereignty issue*, or just siding with the *will of man aspect* of the Scriptures. This is what it means to be "yet carnal". The apostle Paul spoke of this in 1st Corinthians 3:3, when he stated…"For you are yet carnal: for whereas there is among you envying, and strife, and divisions, are you not carnal, and walk as men?" To be "carnal" in this sense is to still be governed by mere human nature, and not by the Spirit of God. Most remain carnal when it comes to the *issue of sovereignty* and the *will of man*. Instead of rightly dividing God's Word, they pick one side over the other and divide themselves into different categories of belief. Hence, "Calvinism" and "Arminianism" were created by the minds of men who wanted to side either with "Fatalistic Sovereignty" or

"Free Will", both of which contain elements of truth, but are ultimately out of balance in the grand scheme of things. Once again, it will be our goal in this teaching to show a proper and balanced Scriptural view of *God's sovereignty* and *man's will* (which includes his use of God-given authority), as well as the pitfalls of leaning toward the errors of *fatalism* and *free will*.

SOVEREIGNTY VS. FATALISM

According to George Addair:

"By the *sovereignty* of God, we mean the supremacy of God. We mean His Kingship and Headship. It literally means, "The Godhood of God." To declare that God is *sovereign* is to declare that He is God. It is to declare "That He is the most High, doing according to His will IN THE ARMY OF HEAVEN AND AMONG THE INHABITANTS OF THE EARTH, so that none can stay His hand or say unto Him what are You doing?" (Daniel 4:35) To say that God is *sovereign* is to declare that He…"is the Almighty, the possessor of all POWER IN HEAVEN AND EARTH, so that none can defeat His counsels, THWART HIS PURPOSE, OR RESIST HIS WILL." (Psalm 115:3) To say that God is *sovereign* is to declare that He is…"The governor among the nations." (Psalm 22:28) He sets up kingdoms, overthrows empires, and determines the course of dynasties as pleases Him best. To say that God is *sovereign* is to declare that He is…"The only Potentate, the King of kings, and Lord of lords." (1st Timothy 6:15) -end quote- (The Absolute Sovereignty Of God, George Addair)

I think it is safe to say that God is in charge, and that *He is runnin' this thing!* Having said all of this, though, has God made no provision under the umbrella of His *sovereignty* to extend to man a *will*, with which he (man) can make *choices*, and be given the opportunity to operate in *authority, responsibility, accountability, and stewardship*? Those who hold the view of "Fatalism" would surely answer no to the previous question, but it is at this time that we will expose the error of the "fatalistic view".

According to Dr. Stephen Jones:

"A *fatalist* is one who sees God as *sovereign* without understanding the *authority* that God gave man. With such an unbalanced view, the *fatalist* can always blame God for everything and take no *responsibility* upon himself for his actions. He can always justify any sin that he does by saying, "Well, God is sovereign; therefore, I had no choice but to do it." *Fatalists* do not really understand that there is a judgment to come, where every man will be judged according to his works (Rom. 2:6; Rev. 20:12, 13).

To keep from being a *fatalist*, one must clearly understand the difference between the *will* **(thelema)** and the *plan* **(boulema)** of God. This is best illustrated by the real-life example of Pharaoh, who could and did resist the *will* of God by his *authority*, but could not resist the *sovereign plan* of God. Secondly, we have the example of Israel being held *accountable* for refusing to enter the Promised Land, even though God had withheld from them a heart to know, eyes to see, and ears to hear (Deut. 29:4). In that case, the judgment was limited to 40 years - the extent of their *authority*." -end quote- (How To Believe In God's Sovereignty Without Being A Fatalist, Dr. Stephen Jones)

While the "Fatalistic View" exalts the idea of the *sovereignty* of God, it robs us of the blessings that are to be associated with *obedience* to the *will* **(thelema)** of God in the here and now. It also tears down what is at the very heart of God and His Kingdom, in that it does not recognize God-given *authority* to man and our *responsibility* to take what God gives us and to bring forth fruit to the glory of God. *Fatalism* does have its pitfalls that need to be exposed, especially for those who are to be *leaders* in the Kingdom of God. In order to be a *leader* (not just a citizen) in God's Kingdom we must understand the principles of *sovereignty* as well as *authority*.

This is the whole point of our training by God. We are being raised up to be an overcomer to lead the nations into the righteousness of God. How could we possibly be able to lead God's people if we do not grasp the notion of *authority* and how to distribute what God has deposited in us to the people? The end product of *authority* is to become a king and a priest. This enables us to have power with God and power with the people. In other words, we will go to God on behalf of the people, and we will go to the people on behalf of God. It would be impossible to do this if we just viewed ourselves as robots and puppets on a string, controlled by the *fatalistic grip* of a God Who forced our every action. Yes…it is true that no one can withstand, overturn, or stop the *plan* **(boulema)** of God from coming to pass, and thank God for it, because God's *plan* will result in the salvation of all men in the fullness of time. But this does not mean that we are exempt from our duty to obey the *will* of God and to nurture and distribute God-given *authority*.

AUTHORITY VS. FREE WILL

It is imperative for those who are leaders in God's Kingdom to understand their call to *authority*. As we stated earlier, there are general citizens in God's Kingdom, and then there are leaders that emerge that have ears to hear and enter into the training process of sanctification. For God's leaders it is all about learning to be *harnessed* by the Lord, which speaks of a willing submission to the *sovereignty* of God. As we submit to God and partake of His divine nature He begins to give us *power / authority*. What we do with this *power* and *authority* determines whether God gives us more or keeps us where we are at. The definition of *authority* is: the *power* to determine, adjudicate, or otherwise settle issues or disputes; jurisdiction; the right to control, command, or determine. Along with *power* and *authority*, we will also be given opportunities to exercise *responsibility*, *accountability*, *stewardship*, and the ability to make certain *choices*. Let us examine the Scriptures to support these claims.

Matthew 28:18 (New International version):

¹⁸Then Jesus came to them and said, "All **_authority_** in heaven and on earth has been given to Me."

Note: This is proof of God's intention to give *authority* to His leaders. Jesus was the Pattern Son of God. If He was given *authority* by the Father, then so shall we be given *authority*. Jesus was The Son of God to bring many sons unto glory. Since all *authority* belongs to Him, He is the One Who gives it to His leaders to use to gather in the nations of the world.

Revelation 2:26-27 (New International Version):

²⁶To him who overcomes and does My will to the end, I will give **_authority over the nations_**. ²⁷He will rule them with an iron scepter; he will dash them to pieces like pottery just as I have received authority from My Father.

Note: Here we are able to see the transfer of the *authority* of Jesus Christ to His overcomers to be distributed in the form of ruling the nations. Surely those who play a part in the fullness of this manifestation of *authority* are those who were faithful to accept it and use it in a proper way when a measure of authority was given to them in part. It is evident in this Scripture passage that a leader in God's Kingdom must recognize, submit to, and demonstrate *authority*.

Luke 12:42-48 (New King James Version):

⁴²And the Lord said, "Who then is that _**faithful**_ and _**wise steward**_, whom *his* master will make _**ruler**_ over his household, to give *them their* portion of food in due season? ⁴³Blessed *is* that _**servant**_ whom his master will find so doing when he comes. ⁴⁴Truly, I say to you that he will make him _**ruler**_ over all that he has. ⁴⁵But if that _**servant**_ says in his heart, 'My master is delaying his coming,' and begins to beat the male and female servants, and to eat and drink and be drunk, ⁴⁶the master of that _**servant**_ will come on a day when he is not looking for *him*, and at an hour when he is not aware, and will cut him in two and appoint *him* his portion with the unbelievers. ⁴⁷And that _**servant**_ who knew his master's will, and did not prepare *himself* or do according to his will, shall be beaten with many *stripes*. ⁴⁸But he who did not know, yet committed things deserving of stripes, shall be beaten with few. _**For everyone to whom much is given, from him much will be required; and to whom much has been committed, of him they will ask the more.**_"

Note: This is an extremely informative passage of Scripture which actually sheds much light on several topics. First and foremost, it testifies to the fact that God has *three different harvests* in which He shall draw (drag) all men unto Himself through Jesus Christ. The three harvests are: *The Overcomers, The Church In General*, and *The Unbelievers*. Secondly, it speaks of *faithfulness* and *stewardship*. Keep in mind that a *steward* is a *manager* of affairs, whether it consists of a farm, household, land, or finances. This person is an *overseer* and *caretaker*, and has obviously been given a measure of *authority*, with which they will ultimately have to answer to God for.

Going back to the Scripture passage, the <u>overcomer</u> (faithful servant) is obviously faithful to the call and recognizes the *authority* given by God and takes great care to become a *wise steward* with the blessings (*power, authority*, and *revelations*) he has received from God. The <u>church in general</u> (speaking of those who are justified, but not sanctified in their behavior and character) is deemed to be an unfaithful servant and is destined and appointed to have its portion with the <u>unbelievers</u>. These two categories (the church in general / unbelievers) are those who are still in need of correction in order to fully recognize and submit to the *authority* of Jesus Christ - the church in general in regard to sanctification, and the unbelievers in regard to justification and sanctification. The overcomers are destined for *rulership*, because of their attitude toward God and *authority*, while the church in general and the unbelievers are destined for further correction, due to their lack of commitment to *authority*, whether through disobedience or ignorance. There is obviously a huge difference, though, as far as the church in general and an unbeliever. Their judgments will be different as well.

Finally, the stripes that are spoken of in this parable refer to levels or degrees of punishment for the purpose of correction. This language (beaten with many or few stripes) is "hyperbole" (used to evoke strong feelings or create a strong impression). While it most likely does not refer to literal stripes, it surely refers to the severity of correction to be administered upon those who have yet to recognize Jesus Christ as Savior and Lord, whether through disobedience or ignorance. The overall meaning of this parable, even though it comes across as a *tad* harsh to the minds of men, is actually one of restoration and love coupled with correction. It exalts God as a loving Father Who will not only harvest all souls unto Himself, in the order of overcomers, the church in general, and the unbelievers, but will also correct every one of us through judgment. Yes…there is a righteous and remedial purpose to the judgment of God! What makes this passage of Scripture *so powerful* is that it incorporates all the elements we have been speaking of:*power, authority, responsibility, accountability, stewardship*, and the ability to make certain *choices*.

1ˢᵗ Corinthians 4:1-2 (Amplified Bible):

¹So then, let us [apostles] be looked upon as ministering servants of Christ and **stewards (trustees) of the mysteries (the secret purposes) of God**. ²Moreover, **it is [essentially] required of stewards that a man should be found faithful [proving himself worthy of trust].**

Note: I can think of no greater gift from God than to be given an understanding of HIS MYSTERIES! Once He reveals Himself to us along with *His secret purpose of the ages*, we are then *responsible* and *accountable* to Him for this knowledge. The apostle Paul referred to it as **the spirit of wisdom and revelation in the knowledge of God** (Ephesians 1:17). Paul said we actually become a steward (trustee) of these mysteries. What an honor…a privilege…an amazing gift! So many great men and women in this life seek for wisdom, knowledge, meaning, and the answer for why we are here and what "it" is all about, but yet so few actually discover the mysteries of the Kingdom of God. As I write this I am fully aware (at least I hope so) that unless God first reveals Himself to us in and through His Word to uncover His mysteries to us that it is hopeless on our end to discover His secret purpose. In simple terms, God must make the first move to help us to see what we are not able to see.

Having said all of this, though, God gives us further revelation based on what we do with the amount of revelation that He initially gives us. For example, if we are good stewards of what He gives us, then He gives us more…and more…and so on. Is this not how we raise and teach our own children? If we give them a privilege and they respond in a grateful and responsible manner, then are we not more than pleased to extend further privileges to them? But on the other hand, if we give them a gift or a privilege and they show no concern or abuse what has been given to them, then are we not apt to remove both the current and even future privileges for the time being?

I cannot stress enough just how magnificent a gift it is to receive revelation from God concerning His mysteries. There is nothing greater in this life…nothing! The amount of gratefulness, emphasis, care, and concern to nurture and develop the mysteries that God reveals to us plays a part in whether or not God gives us more or keeps us right where we are in our understanding of Him. What *value* do we place on receiving revelation from God? Do we say…Oh… o.k. …it is *neat* to know the mysteries of God, but what's the big deal? Or do we say…I cannot believe how incredible it is that God would choose *me* to reveal His mysteries to, and that He has had so much mercy on *me* to help *me* see Who He really is and what He has truly accomplished for the human race…thank you God for revealing Your mysteries to me!

Who would you rather give all of your most prized possessions to? Would you give them to someone who could care less, or would you give them to someone who showed so much interest they would rather die unless they could have the opportunity to receive such gifts? Revelation from God is a tell-tale sign of where a person is in their relationship with Him, and is proof of what value they place on God and His Kingdom. As well, revelation from God summarizes everything we have been speaking of in reference to *sovereignty* and *authority*. It takes the *sovereignty* of God to have His mysteries revealed to us, but if we do not recognize that *authority*, *stewardship*, and *faithfulness* are **required**, then we will remain immature, unsanctified, and void of the character and nature of our Heavenly Father.

Matthew 25:14-30 (New International Version):

¹⁴"Again, it will be like a man going on a journey, who called his servants and ***entrusted his property to them***. ¹⁵To one he gave five talents [probably about $5,000], of money, to another two talents, and to another one talent, each according to his ability. Then he went

on his journey. ¹⁶The man who had received the five talents went at once and put his money to work and gained five more. ¹⁷So also, the one with the two talents gained two more. ¹⁸But the man who had received the one talent went off, dug a hole in the ground and hid his master's money. ¹⁹After a long time the master of those servants returned and settled accounts with them. ²⁰The man who had received the five talents brought the other five. 'Master,' he said, 'you entrusted me with five talents. See, I have gained five more.' ²¹His master replied, 'Well done, good and faithful servant! You have been faithful with a few things; I will put you in charge of many things. Come and share your master's happiness!' ²²The man with the two talents also came. 'Master,' he said, 'you entrusted me with two talents; see, I have gained two more.' ²³His master replied, 'Well done, good and faithful servant! You have been faithful with a few things; I will put you in charge of many things. Come and share your master's happiness!' ²⁴Then the man who had received the one talent came. 'Master,' he said, 'I knew that you are a hard man, harvesting where you have not sown and gathering where you have not scattered seed. ²⁵So I was afraid and went out and hid your talent in the ground. See, here is what belongs to you.' ²⁶His master replied, 'You wicked, lazy servant! So you knew that I harvest where I have not sown and gather where I have not scattered seed? ²⁷Well then, you should have put my money on deposit with the bankers, so that when I returned I would have received it back with interest. ²⁸Take the talent from him and give it to the one who has the ten talents. ²⁹*__For everyone who has will be given more, and he will have an abundance. Whoever does not have, even what he has will be taken from him.__* ³⁰*__And throw that worthless servant outside, into the darkness, where there will be weeping and gnashing of teeth__*.'

Note: This parable is fairly self-explanatory, so we will not go into too much detail as to the explanation, for it is quite obvious what is being said. I do want to mention a few key points, though. Notice how the master of the parable **_entrusted his property to his servants_**. This terminology clearly speaks of *responsibility*, *accountability*, and *stewardship*. The remainder of the parable simply shows us how two were good stewards of what they had been given, while one was not. The concluding statement of the parable has some very sharp words which paint a picture of how God feels about those who are lazy and have a *couldn't-care-less* attitude toward Him and His gifts. Not only will those who do not recognize their hour and opportunity of *responsibility*, *accountability*, and *stewardship* have their gifts taken and given to another, but they will weep and gnash their teeth in the darkness. The phrase "…into the darkness, where there will be weeping and gnashing of teeth" refers to those who will experience **severe regret**, **sorrow**, and **remorse**, while being exposed to further correction. Darkness is obviously the opposite of light, and is used here to signify the *condition* of those who will experience such regret for not having been a good and faithful servant. Yes…they will eventually be corrected and restored to the Master, but not without having suffered through deep remorse for their inexcusable behavior and attitude toward Him.

Since this article is about the balanced view of God's *sovereignty* and man's *authority*, it is at this time we will discuss *authority* in relation to the term and *so-called* belief of *free will* and offer some concluding remarks. Here are a few words from Dr. Stephen Jones from his article entitled, "How To Believe In God's Sovereignty Without Being A Fatalist"…

"Man's *authority* is NOT the same as "free will", although many have confused the two and have tried to prove "free will" by pointing to Scriptures that establish man's *authority*. Only *sovereignty* has *free will*. Authority is limited. It is my hope and purpose to bring people to a closer balance in understanding how God's *sovereignty* and man's *authority* operate at the same time. This, in turn, could help resolve some of the long-standing doctrinal disputes between the two sides, as well as help people get a clearer perspective of God's ability to accomplish His purposes for the earth - and for each person as an individual.

The quick answer is that *man's authority ends where God's sovereignty begins*. Man has the *authority* to reject God for a time, but ultimately, God's *sovereign will* is going to be fulfilled. Man can reject God and receive judgment, but God's judgment itself will correct his fleshly disposition so that he genuinely submits to Jesus Christ.

We have shown this in other writings, summarized best in the short booklet, If God Could Save Everyone - Would He? There we show that man has *authority* over his own "land" that God has given him as his inheritance; but God yet retains *sovereignty* over him by right of creation. The *authority* that God has given man is limited. **Man does not have the ability to sell himself to the devil (or to the flesh) for ever.** He can do so only within the parameters of time." -end quote- (How To Believe In God's Sovereignty Without Being A Fatalist, Dr. Stephen Jones)

In conclusion, the Biblical facts of the matter are simply this:

God is *sovereign*, but does not force and manipulate our every thought and action, even though He is able to do so. He does at times override our *will*, but not all the time because He wants to teach us how to receive, handle, and use *power, authority, responsibility, accountability, stewardship,* and *choices*. On the other hand, man has *authority* and a *will*, but both are limited. They are not unlimited and totally *free* and to be seen as *sovereign* over God. And THANK GOD that He has not given us an unlimited amount of *authority* and *free will* in our present state with which we would run the risk of consigning ourselves for ever to a lost condition. Remember…we are the property of God. He will not let this happen. God has the final say.

Ladies and Gentlemen…it is as simple as that! This matter is not as complicated as many have made it out to be. God is in control of everything, but gives man an opportunity to experience a measure of His *power* and *authority* and how to use it in the proper way. Those who *pass the test* will be the ones to "pull the King's Carriage" and usher in the manifestation of the sons of God at the appointed time. They will then be a vessel of God's *authority* in the fullness and rule the nations, teaching them the righteousness of God until every knee bows to Jesus Christ and every tongue confesses Him as Lord of all to the glory of God the Father!

PART 7 - ELITE VS. ELECT

There are certain terms, words, topics, and concepts from the Bible, that when spoken or brought up evoke strong negative feelings and immediate reactions, causing the listener to shut down, make surface judgments, and want to hear no more. The words "elect" or "election" are two such words. When the topic of "God's elect" comes up it is usually met with resistance by the minds of men on the grounds that it is associated first and foremost with those of the "Baptist" and "Reformed" persuasions. This is also known as "Calvinism" and it has its roots in the "Augustinian View" of "election". In simple terms, it is the belief system that says that God has chosen to save only a select ("elect") group of people and to damn the rest to an eternal hell forever. In addition to this, many people view the topic of "the elect" (or "election") as a type of "elitism", and *write it off* in their minds because it comes across to them as though it is being stated that the "elect" are an "elite" group of people who think they are better than all the rest. The third reason why the concept of "God's elect" would be rejected is due simply to a "lack of knowledge" concerning what the Bible actually teaches on the subject. It will be our goal in this teaching to address all three points mentioned ("Calvinism", "Elitism", and "Lack Of Knowledge") and to explain what it truly means to be one of "God's elect".

THE CALVINISTIC VIEW OF ELECTION

As was stated in the opening paragraph of this teaching, "Calvinism" has its roots in the "Augustinian View" of "election". "Augustine" taught that God had predetermined some for salvation and some for infinite punishment. This teaching was later embraced and developed by "John Calvin" and came to be known as "Calvinism". In the "Five Points Of Calvinism", it is referred to as "Unconditional Election". Here is the definition of "Unconditional Election" from **Wikipedia, The Free Encyclopedia:**

"*Unconditional election* is the *Calvinist* teaching that before God created the world, He chose to save some people according to His own purposes and apart from any conditions related to those persons. *Unconditional election* is drawn from the doctrines of salvation adopted by *Augustine of Hippo*, was first codified in the Belgic Confession (1561), re-affirmed in the Canons of Dort (1619), which arose from the Quinquarticular Controversy, and is represented in the various Reformed confessions such as the Westminster Standards (1646). It is one of the *five points of Calvinism* and is often linked with predestination." -end quote- (Unconditional Election, Wikipedia, The Free Encyclopedia)

The "Calvinistic View" of "Unconditional Election" was once again carried on later in history by figures such as: Theodore Beza, George Whitefield, Jonathan Edwards, and Charles Spurgeon. Some of the more recent teachers of "Unconditional Election" are: R. C. Sproul, Wayne Grudem, John Piper, Michael Horton, Don Carson, and James White.

The men we have mentioned who have embraced "this idea" of "election" are actually correct in stating that God is sovereign and that according to His sovereignty He "elects" or "chooses" certain people over others. The part of their teaching that is incorrect lies in their understanding and explanation of the ***purpose of election***. They view "election" solely as deliverance from infinite punishment, which teaching is incorrect and not supported by Scripture. The question is not...Does God "elect" certain people? The real question should be...What is the ***purpose of*** *election*? Their error is not in "election" itself, but in the ***purpose of election!***

Note: Some ideas, thoughts, and partial statements from this section (The Calvinistic View Of Election) were incorporated and quoted from **Hope Beyond Hell**, **Gerry Beauchemin**.

Next, we must address the idea of "spiritual elitism" and how it has caused some to *have a bad taste in their mouth* concerning "God's elect". This is another stumbling block we must overcome in order to rightly divide what the Scriptures speak pertaining to the true idea of Biblical "election".

SPIRITUAL ELITISM

Some have divorced themselves from the idea that God has an "elect" company of people He is training (qualifying) to be the leaders of His Kingdom. Those who hold this view somewhere down the line have become *offended* by this concept (that God "elects" a "firstfruits" company of leaders) and found it convenient to dismiss the Biblical idea of "election" by calling it "spiritual elitism". If there is one common error I have personally witnessed over and over again with teachers in the body of Christ, it is this: In an attempt to correct false doctrine that veers off in one extreme or the other, most use the method of going all the way to the other extreme and find themselves (unknowingly) in false doctrine to the opposite extreme.

For example, are there those who think they are "elite" and better than others? Well…yes. Are there those who view Biblical concepts such as "manifest sonship", "he that overcomes", and "the Manchild" as an opportunity to flex their self-righteous Pharisaical muscles on others? Well…yes. Still yet, are there those who would actually teach that "God's elect" are "elite" and better than all the rest of God's children? Well…yes. Having said all of this, though, does the Bible not speak of kings, lords, priests, leaders, rulers, overcomers, the "elect", firstfruits, and the manifestation of the sons of God? Well…sure it does. **Here is where we must be careful to expose the wrong attitude of "spiritual elitism", but also (with the proper balance) uphold and proclaim the true reality and meaning of "God's elect".** Just because some wrongly use the idea of "election" as an opportunity to claim they are "spiritually elite" (which indeed they are not) does not mean we need to take the term "elect" and brand it as something bad, or attempt to say there is no such thing. **No… we must be better stewards of the mysteries of God than that! We must do a better job of rightly dividing the Word of truth than that!**

I am more than happy to expose pride and "elitism" in any who may think they are *the cat's meow*. But I am not going to go all the way to the other extreme and say there is no such thing as those who will qualify to be overcomers and be raised up as leaders in the first resurrection to rule and reign with Jesus Christ. To deny this truth (that God has "elect" overcomers who are the firstfruits / the manifestation of the sons of God) is just as wrong as to claim to be "spiritually elite". They are two ditches of error on either side of the path of truth. One claims to be "spiritually elite", and the other denies the plan of God (which includes a firstfruits harvest **before** the harvests of the church in general and the unbelievers). I am fully aware that the terms "overcomers", "the Manchild", and "manifest sons" will ultimately include all of creation (everyone). But the Bible clearly does not teach this will happen collectively all at the same time. Once again, the Bible explicitly paints a picture of three distinct harvests (the overcomers, the church in general, and the unbelievers) which will ultimately include all, but not all at the same time. It is important we make the distinction between the different harvests, because if we do not, we are not rightly dividing the Word of God. And that is how God would want it, because He is the One Who created these three harvests for a very specific reason and purpose! In essence, to *write off* "election" as "spiritual elitism" is no more than a form of "false humility" and a denial of the plan of God for His creation.

LACK OF KNOWLEDGE

Most Christians are simply unaware, uninformed, and have a lack of knowledge in reference to the fact that God has an "elect" firstfruits harvest, as well as two other harvests pertaining to the church in general and the unbelievers. In simple terms, they just don't know "the plan of God". The modern day church of Jesus Christ has so watered down and diluted the true message of the Gospel that they are hardly able to recognize revelation truth and knowledge when it is presented to them. In fact, they usually fight against what is true (calling it evil), and uphold what is false (calling it good). We have all been in this condition (a lack of knowledge) at one time or another and will probably be there in times to come. So this is not a *put down* to those who have not seen these things or an *ego trip* for those who are able to see more clearly than others. I know personally that except for the grace and mercy of God I would know nothing at all about His glorious plan of the ages for all men. This is why Paul prayed for the church at Ephesus concerning the spirit of wisdom and revelation in the knowledge of God.

Ephesians 1:17-23 (New King James Version):

[17]that the God of our Lord Jesus Christ, the Father of glory, may give to you **the spirit of wisdom and revelation in the knowledge of Him,** [18]**the eyes of your understanding being enlightened; that you may know what is the hope of His calling, what are the riches of the glory of His inheritance in the saints,** [19]**and what** *is* **the exceeding greatness of His power toward us who believe, according to the working of His mighty power** [20]which He worked in Christ when He raised Him from the dead and seated *Him* at His right hand in the heavenly *places,* [21]far above all principality and power and might and dominion, and every name that is named, **not only in this age but also in that which is to come.** [22]And He put all *things* under His feet, and gave Him *to be* Head over all *things* to the church, [23]which is His body, the fullness of Him Who fills all in all.

If we do not understand "the plan of God", then we do not have "the spirit of wisdom and revelation" in the knowledge of God through Jesus Christ. The opposite of this statement is also true, in that if we do not have the "spirit of wisdom and revelation" in the knowledge of God through Jesus Christ, then we do not understand "the plan of God". Paul told us that we needed **revelation (unveiled reality)** and **enlightenment** from the Spirit of God to know and understand: the hope of God's calling, the riches of God's inheritance in the saints, the power of God in this age and the coming age, and the mystery of the church, **which is His body, the fullness of Him Who fills all in all.**

If you are reading this and you are unaware of these things, then you should make it your goal from here on out to simply read the Scriptures with this passage in mind (Ephesians 1:17-23), and by all means…<u>***ASK GOD TO GIVE YOU THE SPIRIT OF WISDOM AND REVELATION IN THE KNOWLEDGE OF HIM!!!***</u> "Ask, and it will be given to you; seek, and you will find; knock, and it will be opened to you. For everyone who asks receives, and he who seeks finds, and to him who knocks it will be opened." (Matthew 7:7-8 NKJV) Having said of all this, we are now in position to ask and answer the most important question pertaining to this topic, which is: **What is the purpose of "election"?**

THE PURPOSE OF ELECTION

The words "elect", "elected", and "election" are used several times in various places throughout the Old and New Testaments. Some examples of Scripture references using these words can be found at: Isaiah 42:1;

Matthew 24:24; Romans 8:33; 1st Peter 1:2; 1st Peter 5:13; Romans 9:11; Romans 11:5-7; Romans 11:28; 1st Thessalonians 1:4; 2nd Peter 1:10. To say that someone is "elect" or that God has "elected" them simply means God **picks, chooses, selects, or blesses** that person. Oh wonder of wonders that God in His infinite wisdom chooses some before others to know Him and to be awakened to their salvation in Jesus Christ. There is little or no debate concerning this truth which has just been mentioned. The real *meat and potatoes*, though, of the understanding of "election" is what is missed by most who claim to understand it and also by those who have not considered this all-important truth as of yet. The part of "election" which is so little understood is its **purpose**. Once the true purpose of "election" is understood all of the pieces of the puzzle come together. It causes the one who knows nothing of "election" to come alive to the truth, while also causing the "Calvinist" to see the folly of their belief in infinite punishment, and finally, it helps that one who has become bitter toward the truth see that in no way do God's **true** "elect ones" think they are "spiritually elite" or better than others.

To say we believe in or understand the truth of Biblical "election" and not grasp the true **purpose** of "election" is to totally miss the meaning, character, nature, and intent of our Heavenly Father. To know the **purpose** of "election" is to know the heart of God. To be blind to the **purpose** of "election", while embracing certain elements of "election", produces a cold and calloused heart toward God. If one remains in this error, it is a "type" of **"being seared with a hot iron"** to the love, purpose, and plan of God. If we read a book that has ten chapters and stop at chapter eight and say that is the end of the book, this is the same as embracing "election", but not reading the rest of the story which tells of its grand and glorious **purpose**. So…now for the rest of the story! Now…for the **purpose** of "election"!

It is at this time that I wish to lean on the words of Gerry Beauchemin, who so eloquently and in simple terms exposes the raw truth to us concerning the **purpose** of "election". Here are a few excerpts from his book entitled, Hope Beyond Hell.

According to Gerry Beauchemin:

"God promised Abraham and his seed that they would be the heirs of the world! (Romans 4:13) With this comes purpose and great responsibility. We, the "elect", are called to "be" a blessing, and not merely to be "blessed"…

"We as a "kind of firstfruits" among His creatures share this distinction with Christ Who is the "firstborn over all creation" (Colossians 1:15). We labor with Him to implore all people to be reconciled with God (2nd Corinthians 5:20). We are preparing now to rule with Him in the coming ages (2nd Timothy 2:12; Revelation 20:6), to govern five or ten cities (Luke 19:17, 19), to sit on thrones governing the tribes of Israel (Matthew 19:28; Luke 22:30), even to rule over all He has (Luke 12:43-44). Our Lord is preparing leaders for that time, and it all depends on our faithfulness now (2nd Timothy 2:12-13). **The phrase "firstfruits", naturally implies there are "second" fruits. Who are they? They are those whom God will reach in "due time", who are not part of the firstfruits. Christ will draw (drag) all to Himself (John 12:32)…**

"He made us sit together in heavenly places in Christ Jesus, that in the *ages to come* He might *show* ("display" WEY/DBY) the exceeding riches of His grace in His kindness toward us in Christ Jesus (Ephesians 2:6-7). To whom does God plan to display the exceeding riches of His grace if not to those in greatest need of it? Why display it to those who have already known and experienced it?...

"We are the firstfruits - the priests and kings who will judge the world and intercede for the ungodly (lost) in this age and the ages to come. **Note, we are not "exclusive" fruits. We are only "first" fruits among many to come.**" -end quotes- (Hope Beyond Hell, Gerry Beauchemin)

To support these statements, refer to the following Scriptures: 1st Corinthians 6:2-3 (the saints will judge the world and angels), Revelation 1:5-6 (Jesus has made us kings and priests), and Revelation 14:4-5 (firstfruits to God).

THE HIGH CALLING OF ELECTION REQUIRES HUMILITY

For those of you reading this I want to make you some promises. First and foremost, I want to promise you on the authority of the true meaning and intent of the Holy Scriptures that the Biblical explanation of "election" has absolutely nothing to do with God selecting some for salvation over others and preparing an eternal torture chamber for the rest who were not "elected". You can go ahead and *junk* the "Calvinistic" portrayal of "election" on the grounds of their unscriptural doctrine of eternal torture. They are right in their acknowledgment of sovereignty and "election", but they totally miss it when it comes to the **purpose** of "election".

Second, just because there are those who do a poor job of representing "God's elect" and come across with a spirit of "elitism", gives us no right to smear and attempt to remove the true teaching of "election" from the pages of the Bible. I can promise you "election" is clearly spoken of in the Bible. While it ultimately includes all men, the first part of God's harvest deals only with the leaders in God's Kingdom. This is not an ego trip. It is the plan of God spelled out in multiple passages and stories in the Bible. Jesus was The Son of God, but He did not think He was "elite" in His flesh. Even so, He had to pave the way and become the Pattern for the sons and daughters of God who would follow in His footsteps. What if Jesus declined His office as The Son of God because He allowed Himself to be deceived into thinking He should not take His role and leadership position as the Captain of salvation because some might think He was making Himself out to be "elite"? Thank God He knew how to be a leader and not consider Himself "elite" and full of pride.

We cannot go all the way to the other extreme and say there is no such thing as "God's elect" - a firstfruits company of leaders to be manifested at the appointed time to lead the rest of the world to Christ. To take this out of our message is to come up with our own plan. Ultimately, this is a denial of sanctification and all that God is doing to conform the soul of man to His image. Rather, the right thing to do is to expose the spirit of "elitism" as a false image of the true definition of "election", and then go on to uphold and support what it really means to be one of "God's elect".

Finally, the best antidote is to replace our lack of knowledge concerning "election" with revelation truth from our Heavenly Father. Simply ask God to reveal to you what it means to be "elected" in Him and how He wants you to handle this calling of leadership before all the world. I can promise you if you ask you will receive, and if you seek you will find, and if you knock the door of understanding will be opened unto you. If you want me to tell you what to pray for I can tell you this: Pray for the spirit of wisdom and revelation in the knowledge of God, and that He would give you **the revelation of Jesus Christ**, not just as a historical figure, but as The Son of God - God manifested in the flesh. In this revelation you will see all things. You will see His manifestation in the flesh, His sacrifice, His purpose with the sons of God, and His redemption of the human race.

I can also promise you that I do not think I am "elite", but I do believe in "election". Neither does anyone else I know think I am "elite". That is for sure! While I am at it, let me continue by saying that if someone thinks they are "elite" I can promise you they will not play a part as a leader in God's Kingdom. God's true leaders are marked by love and humility. They are as little children.

Bill Britton wrote an article entitled, The High Calling Requires Humility. In it, he states…

"If God has called you to be like Jesus in all your spirit, He will draw you into a life of crucifixion and humility, and put on you such demands of obedience, that He will not allow you to follow other Christians, and in many ways He will seem to let other good people do things which He will not let you do." -end quote- (The High Calling Requires Humility, Bill Britton)

If you want to pull the King's Carriage you will have to submit to the harness and training of the Lord. I can promise you it will not make you feel "elite", but just the opposite. Many will look at you as though you are a failure and of very little consequence in the Kingdom of God. Others will get the credit for the time being. They will brag on themselves and their work, and will seem to have unbroken success. They will be honored and put forward. God will let others be great, and will keep you small. This is what it means to be one of "God's elect". It doesn't sound so "elite" now, does it? God carefully takes the time to **crush** His "elect" so that all of their fleshly ways are burned up by taking on His divine nature. Yes…the reward is great, but so is the price that must be paid. As Paul said, you must count it all loss and but dung in order to win Christ (Philippians 3:8). It will cost you everything, even your very life.

And he who does not take his cross and follow after Me is not worthy of Me. He who finds his life will lose it, and he who loses his life for My sake will find it.

Matthew 10:38-39 (NKJV)

PART 8 - POPULAR OBJECTIONS TO THE RECONCILIATION OF ALL THINGS (PART 1)

And, having made peace through the blood of His cross, by Him to reconcile all things unto Himself; by Him, I say, whether they be things in earth, or things in heaven.

The verse quoted above is from Colossians 1:20. It proclaims to all that Jesus Christ has made peace (with the Father concerning the sin debt of the human race) through the blood of His cross. The verse then goes on to state that the result of the cross of Christ shall be a reconciliation of **all things in earth and in heaven**. This triumphant passage begins in verse fifteen (Colossians 1:15-20) as Paul is describing Christ…"Who is the image of the invisible God, the firstborn of every creature." In verse sixteen it goes on to state…"For by Him were **all things created, that are in heaven, and that are in earth**…" So…the same **all things** that were created by God in Christ will be the same **all things** that shall be reconciled to God through the blood of the cross of Christ.

The word "reconcile" means: 1. to cause (a person) to accept or be resigned to something not desired: *He was reconciled to his fate*. 2.to win over to friendliness; cause to become amicable: *to reconcile hostile persons*. 3.to compose or settle (a quarrel, dispute, etc.). 4.to bring into agreement or harmony; make compatible or consistent: *to reconcile differing statements; to reconcile accounts*. 5.to reconsecrate (a desecrated church, cemetery, etc.). 6. to restore (an excommunicate or penitent) to communion in a church.

Putting all of this together, this passage of Scripture (Colossians 1:15-20) is telling us that God (through the blood of the cross of Christ) shall ultimately cause not only **all people**, but **all things** (visible and invisible) to be made friendly to Him. This will surely include the powers of darkness and even Satan himself (the prince of the power of the air, the ***spirit*** that now works in the children of disobedience). In complete harmony with this, the author of the Book of Acts has recorded for us the words of Peter, when he stated…"And He shall send Jesus Christ, which before was preached unto you: Whom the heaven must receive until **the times of restitution of all things**, which God has spoken by the mouth of all His holy prophets since the world began. (Acts 3:20-21) It is here declared that all the holy prophets since the world began have spoken of a restitution (restoration) of all things. Well…case closed… let's break for lunch…or so you would think.

There are currently, and always have been, "popular objections" to the statements I have made. These objections are attempts from the carnal minds of intellectual and religious men to ignore and explain away **direct statements** in the Scriptures which declare the victorious effort and saving work of the Lord Jesus Christ and the blood of His cross. In all of their attempts to resist Jesus Christ as the **actual** Savior of the world, they always quote Scripture out of context, in a perverted and twisted manner, and miss the true meaning and intent of what they quote. They also literalize some of the metaphors of Scripture, to the complete neglect of many other Scriptures, which declare our Jesus as THE SAVIOR OF THE WORLD!

It is now **WITH GREAT JOY** that we will **destroy and dismantle these "popular objections"** that have held captive the hearts and minds of many of God's people, causing them to believe the lie that the blood of the cross of Christ has been defeated, and that the vast majority of the human race will be lost, separated from God, and tortured forever. I have taught on these topics individually in the past, but now in a collective and concise manner they will be organized and brought together for the purpose of exposing the folly of man's "popular objections" to the reconciliation of all things.

In order to deliver those who are *entrenched* in the belief system that God is going to lose the vast majority of the human race to eternal torture, we must become experts and masters in explaining these *Popular Objections To The Reconciliation Of All Things.*

I call these: **"The Big Ten!"**

Here are ten popular objections to the reconciliation of all things that must be understood in their proper light in order to rightly divide the Word of God and untangle the mess that has been left to us by organized religion and the traditions and doctrines of men.

They are:

I. Matthew 25:46

II. The Unpardonable Sin

III. Everlasting, Eternal, For Ever, Even For Ever And Ever

a. *Olam*

b. *Aion*

c. *Aionios*

IV. The Rich Man & Lazarus

V. Hell

a. *Sheol*

b. *Hades*

c. *Gehenna*

d. *Tartaroo*

VI. Fire

a. *Hell Fire*

b. *Unquenchable Fire*

c. *The Lake Of Fire*

VII. Wrath, Torment, Vengeance, Destruction, Judgment, & Punishment

VIII. Few There Be That Find It

IX. Free Will

X. The Powers Of Darkness

Study these topics until your eyeballs fall out, and until you can see the truth concerning what the Bible actually teaches about these subjects. The world is counting on us to be true Bereans in order that we can teach them the truth so they can be **made free!**

No matter what question or objection anyone may ask in reference to the reconciliation of all things it will fall under one of these ten categories.

<u>*This covers it all.*</u>

Enjoy your search!

*Warning: If you decide to continue reading from this point on, the following words could be potentially hazardous to your belief in eternal torture. If not avoided, these words could result in death or serious injury to certain doctrines that you currently uphold to be true. Other side effects may include: being liberated from the traditions and doctrines of men, and crossing the great gulf - from the carnal mind to the mind of Christ. Please read and / or proceed at your own risk. The author is not responsible for any revelation truth that may accompany the reading of this teaching. All praise, glory, and honor belong to the Lord Jesus Christ. In the event that you experience revelation truth,

please call on the name of the Lord immediately to ensure what you have received is accurate. If the situation persists, please rejoice with "joy unspeakable and full of glory", in that you have been delivered from the greatest lie ever told.

*Note: The passage above (while it may contain a hint of sarcasm) is not meant to be disrespectful in any way. It is not sarcasm just for the sake of sarcasm, but rather, it is meant to get the reader's attention and bring to the surface the suppressed issue of eternal torture, which by and large is accepted by most of Christianity without even a second thought as to whether it is the truth or not. If it causes you to think, then it has served its purpose. Elijah used sarcasm when dealing with the priests of Baal (1st Kings 18:21-39), and Jesus constantly used sarcasm when dealing with the scribes and Pharisees, calling them hypocrites, wolves, vipers, blind guides, fools, serpents, snakes, and so on. Jesus used sarcasm to dumbfound the religious leaders of His day, leaving them speechless and sending them away in deep thought. That is the purpose of true spiritual sarcasm from the Lord.

OBJECTION #1 / MATTHEW 25:46

Down through the ages, the *trump card* of those who believe and espouse the teaching of eternal torture has always been Matthew 25:46. It is with this single verse of Scripture that they *hang their hat* and justify the preaching of their "multiplied sermons seeking to prove their tradition that the vast majority of God's human creation will be LOST, finally, irrevocably, and eternally, and not only will they be lost to God forever and ever, but they will be given up to the most sadistic, inhuman, ungodly torments that could be devised by the vilest fiends." (The previous passage in quotations is a quote from George Hawtin) The verse in question (Matthew 25:46 KJV) states…"And these shall go away into everlasting punishment: but the righteous into life eternal."

Those who use this verse to support their belief in endless torture make the claim that if the *punishment* spoken of in this verse is of limited duration, then it must follow that the *life* is of limited duration. And so they (those who embrace endless torture) feel it is an open and shut case. Well…not so fast. Here come the "Bereans" to the rescue! There are at least **three witnesses** against the false interjection of "eternal" punishment that many insert into this Scripture as their interpretation of Matthew 25:46. They are: Matthew chapter 25 is a **"parable"** concerning the judgment of the nations; the Greek word **"aionios"** refers to that which is "of the ages"; and the **"punishment"** (**"kolasis"**) which is spoken of in this verse is a punishment for correction (pruning) and for the *bettering* of the offender.

According to Louis Abbott:

"Matthew 25:31-46 concerns **the judgment of NATIONS**, not individuals. It is to be distinguished from other judgments mentioned in Scripture, such as the judgment of the saints (2 Cor. 5:10-11); the second resurrection, and the great white throne judgment (Rev. 20:11-15). The judgment of the nations is based upon their treatment of the Lord's brethren (verse 40). No resurrection of the dead is here, just nations living at the time. To apply verses 41 and 46 to mankind as a whole is an error. Perhaps it should be pointed out at this time that the Fundamentalist Evangelical community at large has made the error of gathering many Scriptures which speak of various judgments which will occur in different ages and assigning them all to "Great White Throne" judgment. This is a serious mistake. Matthew 25:46 speaks nothing of "grace through faith". We will leave it up to the reader to decide who the "Lord's brethren" are, but final judgment based upon the receiving of the Life of Christ is not the subject matter of Matthew 25:46 and should not be interjected here. Even if it were, the penalty is "age-during correction" and not "everlasting punishment".

"**An argument was introduced by Augustine**, and since his day incessantly repeated, that if "*aionios kolasis*" does not mean "endless punishment", then there is no security for the believer that "*aionios zoe*" means "endless life", and that he will enjoy the promise of endless happiness. But Matt. 25:46 shows the **"eonian chastisement" and "eonian life" are of the same duration-lasting during the eons, and when the eons end, as Scripture states they will (1 Cor. 10:11; Heb. 9:26), the time called "eonian" is past and the life called "eonian" is finished, but life continues beyond the eons, as Paul teaches at 1 Cor. 15:26:** "The last enemy that shall be destroyed is death." That is, the last, the final one in order. How will it be destroyed? First Corinthians 15:22 gives the answer: "For as IN ADAM ALL are dying, even so IN CHRIST ALL shall be made alive." Death is destroyed when ALL have been vivified, or made alive, IN CHRIST. There will then be no more death. Just as life is destroyed by death, so death is destroyed by life. Our present bodies are mortal and corruptible (1 Cor. 15:44-55), but when mankind is made alive IN CHRIST they will be raised immortal and incorruptible." -end quote- (<u>An Analytical Study Of Words</u>, Louis Abbott)

The following is a quote from A. P. Adams addressing the Greek word "kolasis" that was translated as "punishment" in Matthew 25:46 (KJV).

According to A. P. Adams:

"The purpose of punishment is not only the protection of society, and the restraint of the offender, but also his reformation; this latter should be the main purpose of punishment; any punishment that is not conducive to this end is wholly unjustifiable, it is simply an attempt to overcome one evil with a greater evil; - **now to talk about endless punishment, is nonsense, as much as it would be to talk of endless correction, or endless reforming.** You might speak of endless torture, or endless suffering; but endless punishment is not a proper collection of terms at all. I will add that the original word here rendered "punishment" signifies a punishment for the correction and bettering of the individual, hence it could not be endless." -end quote- (Definitions: Eternal, A. P. Adams)

Notice how this verse reads from The New Testament In Modern Speech. It reads as follows…"And these shall go away into **the Punishment of the Ages**, but the righteous into **the Life of the Ages**." (Matthew 25:46, Weymouth New Testament)

What is being discussed here is *punishment* and *life* within the ages of time (of or belonging to the ages). As we know, the Bible teaches the ages will come to an end. Since "punishment" ("kolasis") signifies a punishment for the correction and bettering of the individual, it is ***impossible*** for it to be endless. This is a sure word of interpretation due to the **double witness** within the same verse (that **"aionios"** refers to something **belonging to the ages of time**, and that **"kolasis"** most definitely refers to **correction, which by nature cannot be endless**). The key is in knowing that **God's punishment is for the purpose of correction**, which will naturally mean that when the offender (or nation) is corrected they will be restored to God. The ages were created by God for man to experience Him and to go through changes during this process. Punishment is one of those experiences that takes place during the ages and belongs to the ages. This is why it is always used in conjunction with the Greek word "aionios" (of or belonging to the ages).

JUST BECAUSE PUNISHMENT IS FOR THE PURPOSE OF CORRECTION AND IS TO BE ADMINISTERED WITHIN THE AGES, AND CORRECTION AND THE AGES WILL COME TO

AN END, DOES NOT MEAN THAT THE LIFE OF GOD WILL COME TO AN END. THAT IS NONSENSE! GOD'S LIFE WILL CONTINUE BEYOND THE AGES AS THE SCRIPTURES STATE. WHEN THE LAST ENEMY IS DESTROYED, WHICH IS DEATH (1ST CORINTHIANS 15:26), THERE WILL BE NOTHING LEFT BUT LIFE. AND ALL WILL BE MADE ALIVE IN CHRIST AND GOD SHALL BE ALL IN ALL (EVERYTHING TO EVERYONE)!

AS WELL, JUST BECAUSE THE LIFE OF GOD IS DESCRIBED AS "AIONIOS" ("OF THE AGES") DOES NOT MEAN THAT IT CANNOT CONTINUE BEYOND THE AGES. IT IS BOTH! GOD'S LIFE IS "OF THE AGES" AND "BEYOND THE AGES". THE REASON THE PUNISHMENT DOES NOT CONTINUE BEYOND THE AGES IS DUE TO THE FACT IT IS FOR THE PURPOSE OF CORRECTION, AND THAT WHEN CORRECTION HAS REACHED ITS END GOAL IT IS NO LONGER NEEDED. THE FACT THAT ALL DEATH, INCLUDING THE SECOND DEATH / THE LAKE OF FIRE, SHALL BE DESTROYED GUARANTEES THAT THERE SHALL BE NOTHING LEFT BUT LIFE AND ALL MADE ALIVE IN CHRIST!

<u>Ladies And Gentlemen Of The Jury</u>...Augustine's *attempt* to paint a picture of eternal torture by using Matthew 25:46 as his *trump card* <u>JUST</u> <u>DOES</u> <u>NOT</u> <u>HOLD</u> <u>WATER</u>! It has been clearly and precisely stated that there are **three specific witnesses** against Augustine's view. Christians who jump into this chapter and quote the last verse of Matthew 25 as evidence for endless torment are doing a tremendous disservice to themselves and others, **not even knowing this passage is a *<u>parable</u>*** concerning the judgment of the nations for their "works". **Matthew 13:34 tells us that Jesus ALWAYS spoke in *<u>parables</u>* when He spoke to the multitudes - always!** Once again, the subject matter of this *<u>parable</u>* concerns the judgment of nations and is not addressing whether individuals experienced justification by faith upon believing on the Lord Jesus Christ. May God help us to wake up and may He heal our consciences that have been *<u>seared with a hot iron</u>* to His love for all. He is not the eternal torturer, but He is the compassionate Father of the Prodigal Son, Who awaits the return of all His children once correction has served its purpose.

We have also shown how the words "aionios" and "kolasis" speak of a **correction** "belonging to the ages" which shall end in restoration and life (all being made alive in Christ). **In essence, Matthew 25:46 is one of the strongest verses in favor of the reconciliation of all things in** the dispensation of the fullness of time, due to the fact that the Greek words "aionios" and "kolasis" are linked together in the same verse. There is really no such thing as "eternal" punishment, since "punishment" is for the purpose of **correction**. How would it be possible to "eternally" *correct* someone? Sooner or later the correction serves its purpose and brings about the desired result.

For those of you reading this I want you to ask yourself this question and to be honest with yourself…Why would you punish your child? Would you punish him (or her) just to inflict pain and satisfy your vindictive thirst for revenge? If so…shame on you. Is our God vindictive, or is He corrective? I think if you spend some time searching the Scriptures, praying, and meditating on the purpose of God's punishment, you will see in your heart that **our God is corrective**. It may take you a while to shed your current belief that God is vindictive, but at least open up your heart to the idea that God's punishment is for the purpose of correction and will end with the result of restoration and reconciliation for all! **Jeremiah 10:24 states…**

O LORD, <u>*correct*</u> me, but with <u>*judgment*</u>; not in thine anger, lest thou bring me to nothing.

OBJECTION #2 / THE UNPARDONABLE SIN

According to Gary Amirault:

"We have all heard of the term "the unpardonable sin". You will not find this term in the Bible, at least not in the Greek text. Some Bibles, such as the New Open Bible New American Standard puts headers into the text such as "Scribes Commit the Unpardonable Sin". These headers are not in the Greek text. They have been added by the editors of that particular translation. This is one reason why so-called "study Bibles" often are a detriment rather than a help. The Scofield Reference Bible was among the first to use such techniques. The Pre-trib Rapture teaching was greatly aided by these kinds of additions into Bibles such as Scofields. They clearly "add to the Word of God" as do most "study Bibles." -end quote- (<u>The Power Of Life And Death In A Greek Four Letter Word - Aion</u>, Gary Amirault)

Now that we have established that the phrase "unpardonable sin" is nowhere to be found in the Bible, and that these words are not Scripturally correct, we are able to properly address what Jesus was actually talking about. The topic at hand is not an "unpardonable sin", but it is "the blasphemy against the Holy Spirit". The verses in question that speak of this sin are: Matthew 12:31-32; Mark 3:28-29; and Luke 12:10. We will deal with the verses that are to be found in Matthew and Mark, for the simple reason that they contain more detail than Luke 12:10 and give us a full picture of what the sin is as well as the penalty.

Matthew 12:31-32 (King James Version):

[31]Wherefore I say unto you, All manner of sin and blasphemy shall be forgiven unto men: but the blasphemy against the Holy Ghost shall not be forgiven unto men.

[32]And whosoever speaks a word against the Son of Man, it shall be forgiven him: but whosoever speaks against the Holy Ghost, it shall not be forgiven him, neither in this **world**, neither in the **world** to come.

Matthew 12:31-32 (Rotherham's Emphasized Version):

[31]Wherefore, I say unto you, All sin and profane speaking, shall be forgiven unto men, - but, the speaking profanely of the Spirit, shall not be forgiven; [32]And, whosoever shall speak a word against the Son of Man, it shall be forgiven him, - but, whosoever shall speak against the Holy Spirit, it shall not be forgiven him, either in this **age**, or the **coming (age)**.

Notice how the King James translators used the word "world" in verse 32. This leaves the impression that there is no forgiveness in this world or the world to come. BUT…this is not correct!

According to Ken Eckerty:

"The problem in this verse is the way the KJV (and other modern versions) have translated the Greek word "aion". The KJV translates it as "world", but the more accurate rendition is given to us by Rotherham. The Bible has a specific word for "world" and that is the Greek word "cosmos". However, Matthew here uses the word "aion" which clearly means a "period of time". It is not referring to a place (world), but a period of time (age). This is significant. In this particular passage, the King James translators are giving us the impression that there are two worlds - one on earth and the next one, which is in heaven. While we do not argue that there are two realms (heaven and earth), is this really what the text is saying? If we believe their translation, it certainly seems that whatever this sin is, it can never be forgiven - either on earth or in heaven. But this couldn't be further from the truth of Jesus' words. Jesus is not speaking of heaven and earth, but two consecutive periods of time. Weymouth's New Testament translates verse 32 this way:

And whoever shall speak against the Son of Man may obtain forgiveness; but whoever speaks against the Holy Spirit, **neither in this nor the coming age** shall he obtain forgiveness. -end quote- (The "Unpardonable Sin", Ken Eckerty)

The sin here being spoken of is one to where the Pharisees claimed that Jesus was performing miracles by "Beelzebub" - the prince of evil spirits (Baal-zebub = "lord of the fly"). In essence, they were attributing the work of the Spirit of God to Satan and the powers of darkness. According to Jesus, this is a very serious sin and is referred to as "the blasphemy against the Holy Spirit". It refers to those who have in some way tasted of the power of God and know better than to go against it, but willfully (and knowingly) resist it, even going to the extreme of calling the Spirit of God an evil spirit ("Beelzebub" - the prince of evil spirits).

Contrary to popular belief, though, the penalty (although very severe) is not an "eternal" penalty. It is a penalty that carries with it "no forgiveness in this **age** or the **age** to come". This terminology gives us specific information as to the details of the penalty. The penalty of this sin causes a person to be excluded from the opportunity to be raised in the first resurrection and to be a part of the leadership company of believers who will rule the nations during the Tabernacles Age to come. As well, those guilty of this sin will no doubt undergo a long and severe correction in the final age (the dispensation of the fullness of times / The Age Of The Ages). It is in the final age (The Age Of The Ages) that they will have the opportunity to be corrected, restored, and forgiven. We know this is the case (that there is another age beyond the coming age) because Paul spoke of the age<u>s</u> (plural age<u>s</u>) to come in Ephesians 2:7, when he stated…"That in the **age<u>s</u>** to come He might show the exceeding riches of His grace in [His] kindness toward us through Christ Jesus."

The very fact that this sin (the blasphemy against the Holy Spirit) is not to be forgiven in **this age or the age to come** (but Paul speaks of **age<u>s</u> to come**) is a testament to the exceeding riches of God's grace and His kindness. God has a built-in **mercy factor**, in that He has framed the ages in such a way that He is able to administer a "just penalty" for sin, and at the same time still bring the sinner to a place of restoration through correction, causing them to come to the saving knowledge of Christ and Him crucified. This is all made possible by the blood of the cross of Christ, which ensures the eventual salvation of all in the fullness of time.

The verses to be considered next are to be found in Mark 3:28-29. As before, we will take into account how they read from both the King James Version and also Rotherham's Emphasized Version.

Mark 3:28-29 (King James Version):

²⁸Verily I say unto you, All sins shall be forgiven unto the sons of men, and blasphemies wherewith soever they shall blaspheme:

²⁹But he that shall blaspheme against the Holy Ghost has **never forgiveness**, but is in danger of **eternal damnation**.

Mark 3:28-29 (Rotherham's Emphasized Version):

²⁸Verily, I say unto you - All things shall be forgiven unto the sons of men, - the sins and the profanities wherewithal they shall profane;

²⁹But, whosoever shall revile against the Holy Spirit, has **no forgiveness, unto times age-abiding**, - but is guilty of an **age-abiding sin**:

According to Ken Eckerty:

"Now take a look at the differences here. In verse 29, the KJV says, "never has forgiveness". Amazingly, the King James translators didn't even bother to include the Greek word "aion" in their translation of this verse, which is most assuredly found in the Greek text. Rotherham (and many other literal translations) accurately translates this. Check out any Greek Interlinear to prove if this is correct. The word "aion" is in the Greek text, but is completely omitted by the King James translators. Why is this? Well, either they were imperfect translators (which they were) or they understood that the word "aion" would put a limit on this unforgiveness, which would contradict their strong belief in the doctrine of never-ending punishment. This verse should be translated, "….has no forgiveness unto times age-abiding." Just as in the first passage we looked at, the unforgiveness spoken of here will only last for two distinct periods or ages - "this age" and "the age to come".

There are two other mistranslations in verse 29. The first is the word "eternal". The Greek word used is "aionios" which comes directly from the noun "aion". Like the noun, this adjective simply means "lasting for an indeterminate period of time". Rotherham translates this as "age-abiding" and Young's Literal uses the phrase "age-during". The second inaccuracy is the word "damnation". Most good Bible versions more accurately translate the Greek word "krisis" to mean "judgment" or "condemnation" not "damnation". This word "damnation" should not be in our Bibles, period! This was an invention of the dark ages in which fear was used to keep the masses under the authority of the Roman Church. In fact, I believe the KJV is the only modern version today that still uses that word in its pages." -end quote- (The "Unpardonable Sin", Ken Eckerty)

While there is so much more that could be said on this topic, as to the nature of the sin and the specific details surrounding the penalty to be associated with it, *suffice it to say* for now that we have exposed the common error to be associated with this sin, in that many refer to it as "unpardonable" accompanied with "eternal" consequences, which is just not the case!

Ladies And Gentlemen Of The Jury…We can be confident in knowing that there is no such thing as an "eternally unpardonable sin" with our Heavenly Father. On the other hand, in no way are we trying to insinuate that sin (or this particular sin) is something we want to engage in. This is not a license to sin, but rather, it is the true interpretation of the Scriptures from the original language. Knowing these things will cause us to want to serve God all the more. Just think about your Savior Jesus Christ and how POWERFUL the blood of His cross truly is. He is able to correct and save to the uttermost, **even reaching to those who are guilty of blasphemy against the Holy Spirit**.

OBJECTION #3 / EVERLASTING, ETERNAL, FOR EVER, EVEN FOR EVER AND EVER

Contrary to what many believe or understand, the Bible is a Book that primarily speaks to us concerning the *ages* of time. It was given to man by God in time and speaks to us about knowing God in time - the *ages* (or *eons*). When it declares the need for wrath, vengeance, judgment, and punishment, it also refers to these attributes that flow out of the love of God, which are corrective in nature, as being part of time and taking place within the confines of time - the *ages*. The key to deciphering all of this is in knowing that there is a difference between time and eternity. "Time" was created by God and has a beginning and an end. "Eternity", on the other hand, is characterized by **timelessness** that simply **is** and has no beginning and no end.

According to J. Preston Eby:

"I am compelled to state that the Bible says very little by way of a definition of eternity because the Bible is essentially a Book of time and for time. It was written for man who lives in a temporal state and who is not yet a totally eternal being. Only as we enter that *state of being* called eternity…only as HE Who IS ETERNITY becomes "All in All" in us…only as we are spiritually metamorphosized into our eternal condition…only as eternity becomes an absolute reality to us…only then will formerly temporal beings such as we now are truly comprehend and understand eternity and things of an eternal nature. This marvelous work has now begun within our spirit as our spirit has been quickened by His Spirit. I stated that the Bible is relatively silent about what eternity is; that is not to say that human teachings and theology haven't taught us a great deal about eternity, but, alas! Much of it over the past centuries has come from the carnal minds of Babylonish theologians and not from the mind of the Eternal One via the Holy Spirit.

ETERNITY IS A STATE OF ABSOLUTE TIMELESSNESS, not of unending time. Eternity is a STATE OF BEING, resident in the very nature and person of God in which such concepts as past, present, future, before, after, change, transition, growth, decay, etc. do not exist. It is wrong to assert that, when time ends, eternity will begin, because eternity has no beginning. Neither did it end when time began, as so many charts indicate. **Therefore it is very important that we make a clear distinction between ages, which belong to time, and eternity, which is timeless. It is more important still that we, in our study of the Bible, search out diligently those passages which refer to time and those which refer to eternity.** Do you have it yet? Do you see? Time is not part of eternity; eternity is not composed of segments of time. Eternity is not time standing still; it is simply not time at all. Eternity doesn't go on and on and on, *ad infinitum*. Eternity doesn't go anywhere, nor does it do anything. Eternity simply IS. Eternity is part of the very nature and person of God. Eternity transcends beyond our knowing anything having to do with time. It is not time at all. It is just a glorious experience of BEING! Eternity simply IS, just as God simply IS. Jesus said, "Before Abraham was, I AM" (Jn. 8:58) - not "Before Abraham was, I WAS." There are not past or future tenses in eternity. There is only one eternal NOW." -end quote- (Eternity, J. Preston Eby)

Notice what J. Preston Eby mentioned (among other things) in the quoted passage above: **"Therefore it is very important that we make a clear distinction between ages, which belong to time, and eternity,** which is timeless. It is more important still that we, in our study of the Bible, <u>**search out diligently those passages which refer to time and those which refer to eternity**</u>." -end quote-

Eby has set us on the right path, in that we must <u>**search out *diligently* those passages which refer to time and those which refer to eternity**</u>. In addition to this, though, there is one other thing we must know before we attempt this all-important search. It is this: *Houston, we have a problem!*

My good friend Chris Dantin told me to never give someone a solution without first showing them they have a problem. You see…we cannot really appreciate or even understand the solution we have been given until we can first see that we have a problem that needs a solution. Once we are able to see the problem, then we will attack the problem with the solution that has been given to us and solve the *conundrum* (an intricate and difficult problem).

In simple terms, the problem we are facing is this: **Many modern Bible translations have done a poor job of translating the words "olam", "aion", and "aionios".** This has caused two major problems for those of us who read these translations and try to come away with a clear picture of God's plan for man. The first problem is that the English words "everlasting", "eternal", "for ever", and "even for ever and ever", have been used in conjunction with English words like "punishment", "judgment", and "destruction". This faulty translation has left readers with the impression that God is going to endlessly "punish", "torture", "destroy", and "torment" the vast majority of the human race. The second problem that has been created is that the Biblical references in the original languages of the Bible to the five ages mentioned are *hopelessly clouded* in most translations.

Yes…the Bible speaks of *at least* five ages. It speaks of past age<u>s</u> (2), this present age (1), and the age<u>s</u> (2) to come. Once we are made aware of this amazing truth, the story of God and His dealings with man takes on a whole new meaning. In Hebrews 1:1-2 (according to the King James Version) it says…"God, Who at sundry times and in divers manners spoke in time past unto the fathers by the prophets, has in these last days spoken unto us by His Son, Whom He has appointed heir of all things, by Whom also He made the **worlds**…" The word "worlds" in verse two comes from the Greek word "aion", and should not be translated as "worlds", but rather, should be translated as "ages".

Here is how Hebrews 1:2 reads in Rotherham's Emphasized Bible, which states..."At the end of these days, He has spoken unto us in His Son, - Whom He has appointed heir of all things, through Whom also He has made the **ages**..." Do you see how **big** of a difference that makes when this word "aion" is either mistranslated or properly translated? It makes all the difference in the *world*! This is what is meant when we say...The Biblical references in the original languages of the Bible to the five ages mentioned are *hopelessly clouded* in most translations. Well...it is our job as Noble Bereans to *uncloud* what has been *clouded*. And that we shall do...by uncovering the meaning of three words: "olam", "aion", and "aionios". Isn't it exciting to know that God has made the **ages**?

OLAM

According to C. Gary Reid and Ernest L. Martin:

"The word *"olam"* is derived from the primitive root *"alam"*, meaning to veil from sight, to conceal. An analysis of the passages where *"olam"* appears shows clearly that the word does not express "eternity" or "everlasting" as it has been frequently translated in the King James Version. Rather, it simply expresses a duration, a time during which a person, thing, or state of a thing exists - literally an age of time which has a definite beginning and conclusion. The duration of an age in Scripture is sometimes defined and sometimes undefined. *"Olam"*, including its usage in the singular and plural and with prepositions and negatives, is translated differently in the Old Testament of our English Version. These various translations with their number of occurrences are tabulated below:

"for ever and ever"	24 times
"from everlasting to everlasting"	4 times
"for ever"	251 times
"everlasting"	60 times
"of ancient times" or "of old time"	2 times
"of old" or "ever of old"	16 times
"world without end"	1 time
"never"	16 times
"perpetual"	22 times
"evermore"	15 times
"old" or "ancient"	13 times
"of" or "in old time"	3 times
"always" or "alway"	5 times

"anymore"	2 times
"world"	2 times
"continuance"	1 time
"eternal"	1 time
"lasting"	1 time
"long time"	1 time
"at any time"	1 time
"since the beginning of the world"	1 time
"ever"	4 times
"long"	2 times
Total occurrences of *olam*	**448 times**

The Time Periods for Salvation, Part 1

by C. Gary Reid and Ernest L. Martin, Ph.D., 1975 Typeset and footnoted by David Sielaff, November 2004" -end quote-

The following is an excerpt from: (The Power Of Life And Death In A Greek Four Letter Word - Aion, Gary Amirault)…"While studying this Hebrew word "olam", I came across some quotations from leading scholars which began to give me much understanding. The classical Wilson's Old Testament Word Studies by William Wilson gives as the meaning of "olam", "duration of time which is concealed or hidden", in other words, an unknown length of time. This unknown length of time could be 3 days and nights as in the case of Jonah, or the length of a man's life, or as long as the period of time the Aaronic Priesthood was in effect, which was around 1,600 years. Well, that seemed to solve all the problems. This definition took care of all the clear contradictions between the Old and New Testament and got old Jonah out of "hell forever". From Jonah's point of view, while he was in the fish, he didn't know how long he was there since he couldn't see the sun and moon. (They didn't invent Timex watches until a few thousand years later.) But while the problem was solved in the Old Testament, it presented some different problems in the New Testament. The Greek equivalent for the Hebrew *"olam"* is the word *"aion"*. We get the English word *"eon"* from this word. It seems that many Bible translators carried the error of mistranslating *"olam"* to the Greek word *"aion."* -end quote- (Gary Amirault)

This brings us to our next stop on our journey through the ages. We will consider the Greek word "aion" next, giving its meaning, and showing how it too has been grossly mistranslated in many leading "selling"

English translations. We are now beginning to see…THE PURPOSE OF THE AGES COME TO LIGHT!

AION

According to C. Gary Reid and Ernest L. Martin:

"The noun *"aion"* means "age" or "eon" and is found 128 times in 105 passages of the New Testament. It doubly occurs in 23 of the 105 passages. In its simple form (noun only), it is found 37 times and with prepositions 68. *"Aion"* is translated as follows in the Authorized Version:

Usage	Number of Occurrences	Representative Scripture
Age	2	Ephesians 2:7
Course	1	Ephesians 2:2
World	40	Hebrews 6:5
Ever	72	Jude 13
Never	7	John 11:26
Evermore	4	2 Corinthians 11:31
Eternal	2	1 Timothy 1:17

Here are seven different renderings of the word *"aion"* as it appears in the form of a noun. On the surface, it seems that the translators were confused as to the right meaning of this important word. The word "world" in the English language is used to describe the present arrangement of human life and activity, but it certainly indicates a terminable period. It had a beginning and will have an end. Indeed "world" conveys no duration of time whatever. Yet *"aion"* shows "time" - though the time is always indefinite as to length. It is just like *"olam"* in Hebrew. The usual words in English which best approximate the original meaning of *"aion"* are "age" and "eon" (the latter word is derived from the Greek original itself)." -end quote-

<u>The Time Periods for Salvation, Part 1</u>

by C. Gary Reid and Ernest L. Martin, Ph.D., 1975 Typeset and footnoted by David Sielaff, November 2004

AIONIOS

According to C. Gary Reid and Ernest L. Martin:

"In the translation of the adjective in the King James Version there is not as much variation. *"Aionios"* is rendered into only four English words.

Usage	Number of Occurrences	Representative Scripture
Eternal	42	Titus 3:7
Everlasting	25	2 Thessalonians 1:9
Ever	1	Philemon 15
World	3	Titus 1:2

The adjective form *"aionios"* cannot carry a force or express a duration greater than the "age" of which it speaks. It cannot mean "eternal" or "everlasting". It literally means "of the age" or "age-long". **Once these meanings of the Hebrew *"olam"* and the Greek *"aion"* are understood, a flood of light will shine forth** to show how God has been using various ages or strategic time periods to perfect His plan of salvation for man." -end quote-

The Time Periods for Salvation, Part 1

by C. Gary Reid and Ernest L. Martin, Ph.D., 1975 Typeset and footnoted by David Sielaff, November 2004

The following is an excerpt from: (The Power Of Life And Death In A Greek Four Letter Word - Aion, Gary Amirault)…"There are some who after wrestling with the facts above will admit that the word *"aion"* means "an age", but they say its adjective *"aionios"* has to mean "eternal" because it is used so often to describe God. Professors in seminaries say these kind of **foolish things**. Anyone with a little bit of sense recognizes that **an adjective cannot have a greater force or meaning than its noun**. "Hourly" cannot mean "yearly", for example. The adjective gets its force from the noun. If the noun *"aion"* means "age", then the adjective *"aionios"* has to pertain to "age" and not to something greater than "age". It cannot therefore correctly represent "eternity". Just because *"aionios"* is used to describe God Who is "eternal" does not mean *"aionios"* means "eternal". God is the God of Abraham, Isaac, and Jacob. Does that mean He is not the God of the rest of us? Of course, not! God can be the God of **ages** as well as being **eternal**. The very nature of God commands the idea of "eternity". He doesn't have to be called "eternal" to make Him "eternal". That is part of His nature. The Bible has many other ways to express "endlessness" or not being exposed to the corruption of death. "Endlessness" is expressed in the Scriptures by the simple phrase "no end" (Luke 1:33; Dan. 7:14; Isa. 9:7). The thought of permanence is also expressed in Hebrews 7:16, "the power of an endless or indissoluble life", and in 1 Peter 1:4, "an inheritance incorruptible, and undefiled, and that fades not away." -end quote- (Gary Amirault)

Once again, as was stated above... **"Once these meanings of the Hebrew *"olam"* and the Greek *"aion"* (along with *"aionios"*) are understood, a flood of light will shine forth to show how God has been using various ages or strategic time periods to perfect His plan of salvation for man."** Having an understanding of these three words ("olam", "aion", and "aionios") will put to rest the idea that God's intentions are to "eternally" punish and torture the vast majority of the human race. This study will also clear up the false idea that God's wrath, vengeance, destruction, judgment, and punishment is *everlasting, eternal, for ever, even for ever and ever.*

Ladies And Gentlemen Of The Jury...The information we have presented is undeniable, and is in favor of the fact that God's dealings with man -- including wrath, vengeance, destruction, judgment, and punishment -- are of a limited duration, i.e., of the ages. There is no way to deny the material that has been presented here, unless the reader chooses to leave the realm of scholarly study and common sense. To be in denial of these facts is to be in denial of the purpose and plan of God, as well as the character and nature of God, which IS LOVE and CORRECTION, and ends in restoration and reconciliation!

OBJECTION #4 / THE RICH MAN & LAZARUS

THE RICH MAN AND LAZARUS / PART 1

IT IS A PARABLE!

The first and most important thing that we must see concerning the story of The Rich Man and Lazarus is: IT IS A PARABLE! A "parable" is: a short allegorical story designed to illustrate or teach a spiritual truth, religious principle, or moral lesson.

Matthew 13:34 tells us that **"Jesus spoke to the multitudes in parables (figurative language); and without a parable did He not speak unto them: That it might be fulfilled which was spoken by the prophet, saying, I will open My mouth in PARABLES; I will utter things which have been kept secret from the foundation of the world."** With this in mind, we can now approach the teachings of Jesus in a proper way. Remember...Jesus always spoke in parables when He opened His mouth in public before the multitudes.

Starting with Luke chapter fifteen Jesus begins to speak a five-part parable. Notice who His audience is. He is speaking to the: publicans, sinners, Pharisees, and scribes. The five parables are:

1. THE LOST SHEEP

2. THE LOST COIN

3. THE TWO LOST SONS (THE PRODIGAL SON)

4. THE UNJUST STEWARD

5. THE RICH MAN AND LAZARUS

The first three parables are spoken to encourage the publicans and sinners concerning God's love for them. The last two parables are spoken to warn the Pharisees and scribes (the religious leaders) of God's disapproval of their self-righteous behavior, which would ultimately lead to the Kingdom of God being stripped from the Jews and given to the Gentiles.

The reason it is so important that we understand that Jesus spoke to the multitudes in parables is because of this: **Many people literalize things in Scripture that are to be understood spiritually, or in a metaphoric sense**. This is the MISTAKE that is often made by most concerning the parable of The Rich Man and Lazarus. We must also understand that the meaning of a parable is LOCKED to the mind of human intellect, which is the carnal (fleshly) mind.

1st Corinthians 2:14-16 states…"But the natural man receives not the things of the Spirit of God: for they are foolishness unto him: neither can he know them, because they are spiritually discerned. But he that is spiritual judges all things, yet he himself is judged of no man. For who has known the mind of the Lord, that he may instruct Him? **But we have the mind of Christ**…"

THE RICH MAN AND LAZARUS / PART 2

THE MEANING OF THE PARABLE

Now that we have established that the story of The Rich Man and Lazarus is a PARABLE, let us seek to understand its true meaning. The meaning of the parable is as follows:

A CERTAIN RICH MAN: This represents the Jewish Nation as a whole (Judah...More specifically: The Priesthood), for they were spiritually rich in the things of God (Romans 3:1, 2...Romans 9:3-5).

CLOTHED IN PURPLE AND LINEN: This statement further clarifies who the Rich Man is, for purple represents royalty, and fine linen represents the priesthood. The Nation of Israel was to be a nation of kings (purple) and priests (linen) before God (Exodus 19:5, 6).

FARED SUMPTUOUSLY EVERY DAY: This once again reaffirms that the Jews were a blessed people, having been given the adoption, glory, covenants, law, service, promises, and of whom as concerning the flesh Christ came (Romans 9:4-5).

A CERTAIN BEGGAR: This represents the Gentiles (Nations) as a whole, for they were spiritual Beggars concerning the things of God (Ephesians 2:11, 12). The Gentiles (Nations) were referred to as the *Uncircumcision*. They were without Christ, being aliens from the commonwealth of Israel, and strangers from the covenants of promise, having no hope, and without God in the world.

LAZARUS: The name "Lazarus" comes from the Hebrew name "Eleazar", which means: "WHOM GOD HELPS". The reason Jesus used the name of "Lazarus" in this parable is for this very reason. The Gentiles (Nations) are those WHOM GOD HAS HELPED.

AT HIS GATE...FULL OF SORES...FED WITH CRUMBS...THE DOGS LICKED HIS SORES: These phrases all point to a description of the Gentiles (Nations), and how they were viewed by the Nation of Israel during the time that Jesus walked the earth. The Gentiles (Nations) were referred to as "dogs", and were considered to be uncircumcised filth by the Jews (Matthew 15:21-28...Mark 7:25-30).

THE BEGGAR DIED: This represents a **change** in the Beggar's condition. The Gentiles (Nations) died to their old condition of a Beggar, and would now be included and brought into the blessings of God (Ephesians 2:13-22).

ABRAHAM'S BOSOM: "Abraham's Bosom" is NOT a physical location. The term represents a place of **spiritual favor and honor**. The Gentiles (Nations) were now given the opportunity to become the children of Abraham. This represented the death of their Beggar status.

THE RICH MAN DIED, AND WAS BURIED: This represents a change in the Rich Man's condition. It signifies the death of Judaism (their religion). We must see that the Rich Man and Lazarus **changed places**. The Rich Man became a Beggar, and the Beggar became a Rich Man. Jesus took the Kingdom from the Jews (the Rich Man) and gave it to the Gentiles (Lazarus…the Beggar…the dogs). (Matthew 21:33-43…Matthew 8:12…Matthew 23:13-39…Mark 12:1-12…Acts 13:46, 47…Luke 13:28, 29).

IN HELL: The English word "hell" (used here) comes from the Greek word "Hades". The word "Hades" simply means: **"the grave, or the place of the dead"**. It carries with it the idea or meaning of **"un-perception"**. The Rich Man, along with his religion (Judaism), was now to be buried, finding himself in a place of un-perception, which refers to not being able to "see" (understand) or grasp the Kingdom of God (John 3:3).

LIFTED UP HIS EYES…IN TORMENTS…SEES ABRAHAM AFAR OFF…LAZARUS IN HIS BOSOM: This represents the Jews suffering the punishment of their sins, in the destruction of their city (70-73 A.D.) and temple, and the sore calamities which have befallen on them ever since. As we now know, the Jews have been through torment for the last 2,000 years due to the rejection of their Messiah. Their religion is dead, and they are currently in un-perception (outer darkness). The Rich Man now sees that Abraham (their spiritual roots) is afar off (cut off), and that Lazarus (the Gentiles / Nations) is in his bosom (a place of favor with God).

FATHER ABRAHAM…MERCY ON ME…SEND LAZARUS… DIP HIS FINGER IN WATER…COOL MY TONGUE…I AM TORMENTED IN THIS FLAME: This is all metaphoric language to show the change of positions and current conditions of the Rich Man and Lazarus. The Jews are now tormented in the flame of having rejected their Messiah. The Rich Man (the Jews) is now asking Lazarus to come and help (comfort) him, whereas before he wanted nothing to do with him, even referring to him as a dog.

THERE IS A GREAT GULF: The great gulf is explained by the apostle Paul in Romans 11:25-36. It is simply this: GOD BLINDED ISRAEL IN PART, UNTIL THE FULLNESS OF THE GENTILES (NATIONS) BE COME IN. Until then, the Rich Man cannot pass from where he is (his condition) to where Lazarus is (his condition), and Lazarus cannot pass from where he is to where the Rich Man is.

SEND HIM TO MY FATHER'S HOUSE...I HAVE FIVE BRETHREN...LEST THEY ALSO COME TO THIS PLACE OF TORMENT: This represents that the Jew learns mercy and compassion after his season of torment. The terminology "five brethren" gives us another undeniable clue as to the meaning of this parable. Modern day Israel, at the time of Jesus, was referred to as Judah. (**Note**: After Solomon died, his Kingdom fell apart - Judah in the South and Israel in the North. What was a strong and united empire broke in two. God divorced Himself from Israel {the Northern Kingdom} in 745 B.C., causing them to be invaded by the Assyrian Empire and deported to the region of Nineveh.) God would later divorce Himself from Judah (the Southern Kingdom) in 70-73 A.D., causing them to be invaded by the Roman Army. This resulted in the destruction of Jerusalem. In this parable, Jesus was speaking to Judah (the Southern Kingdom). He was actually warning them of their destruction that was about to come if they did not repent. It is **extremely interesting** to note that Judah (in the Old Testament) had **FIVE <u>FULL-BLOODED</u> BROTHERS!** They were: **Reuben, Simeon, Levi, Issachar, and Zebulun**. The words "five brethren", used by Jesus, were a direct clue as to the identity of the Rich Man.

<u>MOSES AND THE PROPHETS</u>: This represents the law and the prophets, which could also be said to represent the Old Testament Scriptures. Jesus said...Let them hear them!

<u>IF ONE WENT TO THEM FROM THE DEAD, THEY WILL REPENT</u>: Jesus here alluded to HIS DEATH AND RESURRECTION from the dead, knowing that even though He would rise from the dead, yet would the Jews (as a whole) still not believe and repent.

***<u>NOTE</u>:** Notice how that the Rich Man referred to Abraham as Father, and how that Abraham referred to him as son. This further clarifies the identity of the Rich Man.

<u>Ladies And Gentlemen Of The Jury</u>...Now that we have had our minds renewed (concerning this parable) to the mind of Christ, being brought to a proper understanding of this parable, we can discard the foolish ideas of the traditions and doctrines of men (concerning this parable), which state that this story is about eternal torture in hell. **THAT IS NOT CORRECT!** It is simply a <u>parable</u> which talks about...THE JEWS AND GENTILES!

OBJECTION #5 / HELL - SHEOL, HADES, GEHENNA, & TARTAROO

SHEOL

According to J. W. Hanson:

"That the Hebrew "**Sheol**" never designates a place of punishment in a future state of existence, we have the testimony of the most learned of scholars, even among the so-called orthodox. We quote the testimony of a few:

Rev. Dr. Whitby: "**Sheol** throughout the Old Testament, signifies not a place of punishment for the souls of bad men only, but the grave, or place of death."

Dr. Chapman: "**Sheol**, in itself considered has no connection with future punishment."

Dr. Allen: "The term "**Sheol**" itself, does not seem to mean anything more than the state of the dead in their dark abode."

Dr. Firbairn, of the College of Glasgow: "Beyond doubt, "**Sheol**", like "**Hades**", was regarded as the abode after death, alike of the good and the bad."

Edward Leigh, who says Horne's, "Introduction", was "one of the most learned understanding of the original languages of the Scriptures", observes that "all learned Hebrew scholars know the Hebrews have no proper word for "**hell**", as we take **hell**."

Prof. Stuart: "There can be no reasonable doubt that "**Sheol**" does most generally mean the underworld, the grave or sepulchre, the world of the dead. It is very clear that there are many passages where no other meaning can reasonably be assigned to it. Accordingly, our English translators have rendered the word "**Sheol**" grave in thirty instances out of the whole sixty-four instances in which it occurs."

Dr. Thayer in his Theology of Universalism quotes as follows: Dr. Whitby says that "**hell**" "throughout the Old Testament signifies the grave only or the place of death." -end quote- (The Bible Hell, J. W. Hanson)

Well…There you have it! The word "**Sheol**" means: **the grave, or the place of the dead**. In no way does it denote a place of punishment, torment, or torture. The idea that "**Sheol**" signified a place of punishment entered in through pagan mythology. We are now on our way to understanding the "**hell**" of the Bible. Our next stop on our journey through "**hell**" will be to look at and dissect the Greek word "**Hades**". We will see that "**Hades**" is the Greek equivalent to the Hebrew word "**Sheol**". It is the New Testament word that signifies the grave, or the place of the dead.

HADES

According to J. W. Hanson:

"The Greek Septuagint, which our Lord used when He read or quoted from the Old Testament, gives "**Hades**" as the exact equivalent of the Hebrew "**Sheol**", and when the Savior, or His apostles, use the word, they must mean the same as it meant in the Old Testament. When "**Hades**" is used in the New Testament, we must understand it just as we do ("**Sheol**" or "**Hades**") in the Old Testament.

Dr. Campbell well says: "In my judgment, it ought never in Scripture to be rendered "**hell**", at least, in the sense wherein that word is now universally understood by Christians. In the Old Testament, the corresponding word is "**Sheol**", which signifies the state of the dead in general without regard to the goodness or badness of the persons, their happiness or misery. In translating that word, the seventy have almost invariably used "**Hades**". It is very plain, that neither in the Septuagint version of the Old Testament, nor in the New, does the word "**Hades**" convey the meaning which the present English word "**hell**", in the Christian usage, always conveys to our minds."

Le Clere affirms that "neither "**Hades**" nor "**Sheol**" ever signifies in the Sacred Scripture the abode of evil spirits, but only the sepulchre, or the state of the dead." -end quote- (The Bible Hell, J. W. Hanson)

According to J. W. Hanson:

"That "**Hades**" is the kingdom of death, and not a place of torment, after death, is evident from the language of Acts 2:27, "You will not leave My soul in **hell**: neither will You suffer Your Holy One to see corruption." Verse 31: "His soul was not left in "**hell**", neither His flesh did see corruption," that is His spirit did not remain in the state of the dead, until His body decayed. No one supposes that Jesus went to a realm of torment when He died. Jacob wished to go down to "**Hades**" to his son mourning, so Jesus went to "**Hades**", the under-world, the grave. The Apostle's Creed conveys the same idea, when it speaks of Jesus as descending into "**hell**". He died, but His soul was not left in the realms of death, is the meaning." -end quote- (The Bible Hell, J. W. Hanson)

1st Corinthians 15:55 tells us that "**hell**" ("**Hades**") will be destroyed. It states…"O death, where is your sting? O grave ("**Hades**", "**hell**") where is your victory?" So we can see that "**hell**" ("**Sheol**", "**Hades**") is the grave, or the place of the dead. We can also now see that "**hell**" ("**Sheol**", "**Hades**") is not to endure forever, but is destined to be destroyed. This is also in harmony with Revelation 20:13-14, which tells us that death and "**hell**" ("**Hades**") shall be consumed by the fire of God. This is speaking of the purifying fire of God. AWESOME! O "**HELL**" ("**HADES**", GRAVE), WHERE IS YOUR VICTORY?

GEHENNA / PART 1

(Hope For All Generations And Nations, Gary Amirault)

"Israel, during one part of its history, began to mix the worship of Yahweh with some of the customs of the pagan nations around them. They molded a statue which was half man and half bull. They called this god, MLK. (The original Hebrew had no vowels. One had to put in the vowels from memory.) Some scholars render these three consonants Molock or Molech, others believed it was the word Melech, which means "king" in Hebrew. The latter view would mean that Israel had made an image of Yahweh (their king) in the image of being half man and half animal. Either way, they felt they had *not* abandoned the worship of Yahweh. They felt this new practice was harmonious with the other religious traditions of the Hebrew faith. Regardless of whether he was called Moloch, Molech or Melech, the Israelites took their own babies and placed them in the hands of this statue. Beneath the hands was a pot under which was a very hot fire. The child would fall out of the hands of MLK into the burning pot. As the child screamed with pain, the adults would go into a sexual frenzy as the sounds of the burning children mixed with the beating of drums. MLK was a fertility god. In other Jewish rites, the Jews were commanded to offer up the first-fruits of a harvest unto Yahweh that He might bless the rest of the harvest. The Israelites extended this practice by offering up some of their children as a burnt-offering. Yahweh told Jeremiah the prophet He was going to destroy the city in which they were committing these horrible acts. The location where these rites were performed was in the **Valley of the Son of Hinnom** (also called **Tophet** in the Bible) right outside the Southwest wall of *Jerusalem!*

When speaking of Israel burning their own children, Yahweh said that such a thing never entered His mind. *If God prepared a place in which He was going to torture billions of the human beings He created, how could He say it never entered His mind. Obviously, God never intended, nor ever will eternally burn and torture the men and women He created!* This cruel teaching came from the same place from which Israel got the idea of burning their own children, that is, from a mind which was not subject to the true God; from a depraved mind.

When Jesus in the New Testament used the word which has been incorrectly translated "**hell**" in most Christian Bibles, the place He was referring to was **this valley** in which *Israel* burned their own children, not God. The place called "**Gehenna**" (translated "**hell**") was the Greek form of the Hebrew "**Ge Hinnom**". **This valley** became a disgraceful reminder to Israel of what their forefathers did. **It became the city dump. Jesus warned the very generation in which He lived that if they did not repent, they would find themselves thrown into this valley of garbage which burned night and day.** To tell a Jew something like this was the absolute worst of insult. It meant that their lives were worthless.

A Jew's honor was very important to him, especially at his death. It was not uncommon to hire professional mourners at one's funeral. Imagine paying someone to cry tears at your funeral. This is an example of how vain God's own people were during Jesus' physical presence on earth. Jesus told some of the most religious people of His day, their lives were only fit to be thrown into **the city dump**! What an insult! *And what a prophecy!* The very people who heard these words would find their bodies thrown over the Southwest wall of Jerusalem during the siege against the city in 70AD. Because they did not follow Christ and participated in His crucifixion, their lives truly did become worthless."
-end quote- (Gary Amirault)

Now that we are educated as to the literal history and meaning of "**Gehenna**", understanding that **it is a place on this earth**, let us take a look at **what this literal valley represents spiritually and metaphorically**. FIRST THE NATURAL, THEN THE SPIRITUAL!

GEHENNA / PART 2

According to J. Preston Eby:

"In the New Testament there appears the word "**GEHENNA**" referring to the "**Valley of Hinnom**", or "**Gehenna**", which was **the city dump outside the walls of Jerusalem**, a place of constant burning of refuse. It is interesting to note that those who are pictured as going into "**Gehenna**" are, without exception, not the sinners of the world, but the SINNERS AMONG GOD'S PEOPLE. How precise the type! "**Gehenna**" was **the city dump of Jerusalem**, the Holy City, where every unclean and unnecessary thing was burned and consumed. The antitypical "**Gehenna**" to which our Lord alluded in His teaching is the process of PURIFICATION by which every unclean and unnecessary thing in the lives of His Holy People is purged and consumed by the fires of His judgment. "The Lord Whom you seek, shall suddenly come to HIS TEMPLE…but who may abide the day of His coming? and who shall stand when He appears? for He is like a REFINER'S FIRE, and like fuller's soap: and He shall sit as a refiner and purifier of silver: and He shall PURIFY the sons of Levi (the Priesthood), and PURGE them as gold and silver, that they may offer unto the Lord an offering in righteousness" (Mal. 3:1-3). "**Gehenna**" stands as a type of the place or process of the PURIFICATION OF GOD'S PEOPLE. It is referred to in the Old Testament by the name of "**Tophet**", located in the "**Valley of Hinnom**", a place where many sacrifices were made and dead bodies consumed." -end quote- (Hell, J. Preston Eby)

The idea of God's people being purified in and through fire is also to be found in the apostle Paul's writings. 1st Corinthians 3:12-15 states… "Now if any man build upon this foundation gold, silver, precious stones, wood, hay, stubble; Every man's work shall be made manifest: for the day shall declare it, because it shall be revealed by fire; and the fire shall try every man's work of what sort it is. If any man's work abide which he has built thereupon, he shall receive a reward. If any man's work shall be burned, he shall suffer loss: but he himself shall be saved; yet so as by fire."

This is obviously speaking of a spiritual fire, of which GOD IS! Remember…GOD IS A CONSUMING FIRE (Hebrews 12:29)…Now we can begin to see that Jesus pointed to the literal fire of "**Gehenna**", which did consume literal refuse, to teach us about **the spiritual fire of God**. He used "**Gehenna**" to *typify, symbolize, and portray* what the fire of God was like. HE USED "**GEHENNA**" AS A METAPHOR!

The fire of God is His judgment in our lives that consumes the refuse in us, which is WOOD, HAY, AND STUBBLE! God's fire is for PURIFICATION, **NOT ETERNAL TORTURE!** Nothing was tortured in "**Gehenna**", only consumed and **changed into another form.** Can you now begin to see your <u>FIERY</u> TRIALS as the process in which God is consuming your carnality and CHANGING YOU INTO THE VERY IMAGE OF THE SON OF GOD? As you believe on the Lord Jesus Christ, you are being consumed by the Holy Ghost and FIRE, being changed from glory to glory. This is what "**Gehenna**" represents. It speaks of the ALL-CONSUMING FIRE OF GOD! THANK GOD FOR THE FIRE OF "**GEHENNA**"!

TARTAROO

According to J. Preston Eby:

"Next we consider the Greek word "**TARTAROO**" - the English form is "**Tartarus**". The passage where this word is found is II Pet. 2:4…"God spared not the angels (messengers) that sinned, but cast them down to "**hell**" ("**Tartarus**"), and delivered them into *chains of darkness* to be *reserved unto* judgment." Jude also presents the same truth without mentioning the name as he writes, "And those angels (messengers) who kept not their first position of power and authority, but left their habitation, He has kept *in chains under thick darkness*, for the judgment of the great day" (Jude 6). **The whole thought is of a restraint, a confinement, a prison, a condition in which apostates are held for a specific period of time, in the same manner as prisoners are often held in jail awaiting the day of trial.** "Tartarus" is not the judgment itself, but a state or condition in which persons are inescapably held over unto a day of judgment." -end quote- (<u>Hell</u>, J. Preston Eby)

According to J. W. Hanson:

"Peter alludes to the subject just as though it were well-known and understood by his correspondents. "If the angels that sinned." - what angels? "were cast down to "**Tartarus**", where is the story related? Not in the Bible, but in a book well-known at the time, called the **Book of Enoch**. It was written some time before the Christian Era, and is often quoted by the Christian fathers. But no one can fail to see that the apostle employs the legend from the **Book of Enoch** to illustrate and enforce his doctrine of retribution. As though he had said: "If, as is believed by some, God spared not the angels that sinned, do not let us who sin, mortal men, expect to escape." If this view is denied, there is no escape from the gross doctrine of "**Tartarus**" as taught by the pagans and that, too, on the testimony of a solitary sentence of Scripture! But whatever may be the intent of the words, they do not teach endless torment, for the chains referred to only last unto the judgment." -end quote- (<u>The Bible Hell</u>, J. W. Hanson)

It is believed by many that Peter and Jude were referring to sinning messengers in the days of Noah. These sinning messengers were referred to as "the sons of God" who took "the daughters of men" as wives and produced children by them (Genesis 6:2). As to the nature of these angels (messengers), there are many different thoughts and opinions. Some believe that the flood in Noah's day was brought on and designed by God for the very purpose of thwarting these fallen angels (messengers) in their design.

The important point to see though is that "**Tartarus**" does in no way teach endless torment, for the chains referred to only last **unto the judgment**. It is to be seen as a state or condition in which persons are held over unto a day of judgment for the purpose of correction. The Lord knows how to reserve…THE UNJUST UNTO THE DAY OF JUDGMENT!

<u>Ladies And Gentlemen Of The Jury</u>…

According to J. W. Hanson:

"Canon Farrar truthfully says, in his "Eternal Hope": "And, finally, the word rendered "**hell**" is in one place the Greek word "**Tartarus**", borrowed as a word for the prison of evil spirits not after but before the resurrection. It is in ten places "**Hades**", which simply means the world beyond the grave, and it is twelve places "**Gehenna**", which means primarily, the "**Valley of Hinnom**" outside of Jerusalem in which after it had been polluted by Moloch worship, corpses were flung and fires were lit; and, secondly, it is a metaphor not of final and hopeless but of that purifying and corrective punishment which as we all believe does await impenitent sin both here and beyond the grave. But be it solemnly observed, the Jews to whom and in whose metaphorical sense the word was used by our blessed Lord, never did, either then or at any other period attach to that word "**Gehenna**", which He used, that meaning of endless torment which we have been taught to apply to "**hell**". To them and therefore on the lips of our blessed Savior Who addressed it to them, it means not a material and everlasting fire, but an intermediate, a metaphorical and a terminal retribution." -end quote- (<u>The Bible Hell</u>, J. W. Hanson)

After evaluating the **FACTS**, we can now see that "**Sheol**", "**Hades**", and "**Tartaroo**" speak of literal death (the grave or place of the dead) or the consequences of sin, and "**Gehenna**" was the city dump used in a metaphoric way by our Lord to explain the consuming fire of God.

PART 9 - POPULAR OBJECTIONS TO THE RECONCILIATION OF ALL THINGS PART 2

OBJECTION #6 / FIRE

When discussing the reconciliation of all things with those who are opposed to or in denial of this great truth, one of the main objections used by eternal torture supporters is that the Bible speaks of **fire**, and more specifically: "**hell fire**", "**unquenchable fire**", and "**the lake of fire**". "**Hell fire**", "**unquenchable fire**", and "**the lake of fire**" are often used by many in Evangelical Christianity to strike fear in the hearts of their listeners. The three categories of "**fire**" just mentioned are almost always spoken of in a *literal* sense, and there is little to no explanation of the meaning and purpose of "**fire**" spoken of as it relates to how this word is used throughout the Scriptures. Most claim that the "**fire**" spoken of in these instances is a *literal* "**fire**" that is designed to do nothing more than to torture and inflict pain on individuals, and of course they will say that this condition is to last *for all eternity*. Have you ever *really* stopped and thought about that for a moment? Can you imagine burning someone in a *literal* "**fire**" forever, with no other purpose in mind than to inflict endless and senseless torture? <u>***Wow...that is insane!***</u>

Do we condone this type of behavior as humans in our societies? How would someone be treated or handled if they were to burn someone alive in *literal* "**fire**"? Would this not be a crime and treated accordingly, being condemned by our law enforcement and judicial systems? Surely this type of behavior is vile, to say the least! There must be a meaning and purpose that we are missing when (and if) we speak of "**hell fire**", "**unquenchable fire**", and "**the lake of fire**", and make no mention of the spiritual quality and purpose of this "**fire**".

According to Dr. Harold Lovelace:

"Check again in your Concordance, and you will find verses that read **"Holy Ghost and fire", "hell fire", "unquenchable fire", "ministers a flame of fire", "fiery indignation", "God is a consuming fire", "lake of fire and brimstone", and "the overcomers stand on a sea of glass** mingled with fire". These terms are all from the same Greek word #4442, "pur". **Therefore it is the same fire in all these places**. Now notice that in Mark 14:54 when Peter warmed himself by a "**fire**", it is a different Greek word." -end quote- (Read And Search God's Plan, Dr. Harold Lovelace)

According to J. Preston Eby:

"The word "BURN" means combustion, or to consume. To "consume" does not mean to annihilate, for there is no such thing as annihilation in the absolute sense. When "**fire**" consumes a log in your fireplace it does not destroy any of the elements within the log, it merely *changes their form*. "Combustion" is the process by which chemicals combine to form new chemicals. For example: a tree might be cut down, sawed into fire wood, and burned. When the wood is burning the heat causes the chemicals of which the wood is composed to vaporize, mixing with the oxygen in the air to form new chemicals, including water and the gas carbon dioxide. So what was formerly a tree is no longer identified as the form of a tree, but the substance thereof is now simply CHANGED into a DIFFERENT FORM and exists in its new form within the atmosphere as water, carbon dioxide, etc. **Thus, to "burn", means to CHANGE**. Furthermore, it is interesting to note that "**fire**" does not burn down; it always burns up; it seeks the highest level. And all that it consumes "goes up in smoke", to exist in a new form in a higher dimension. Even if you take a pan of water and place it over a "**fire**", before long the water will take on the property of the "**fire**" and will begin to go up in steam. **To "burn" means to CHANGE, and the change is always UPWARD in its motion**. "FIRE" is the heat and light that you feel and see when something burns. It takes heat to start a "**fire**", but once the "**fire**" is started it produces heat that keeps the process going. Thus, "**fire**" is really HEAT and LIGHT."-end quote- (The Lake Of Fire, J. Preston Eby)

With this in mind, we are now able to see the purpose of God's consuming "**fire**" in our lives. This spiritual "**fire**" (that comes from God) is for the purpose of consuming and destroying the man of sin that is within us. God's "**fire**" works (within us) to consume our wood, hay, and stubble. He burns up our old nature (the propensity within us to sin) by the brightness of His coming (presence). In turn, HIS "**FIRE**" CHANGES US FROM ONE FORM TO ANOTHER. The more we begin to understand the purpose of God's "**fire**", the less we fear it.

HELL FIRE

In Matthew 18:9 (according to the King James Version) the words "**hell fire**" are used. This has caused many to teach and support an *eternal* "**hell fire**" doctrine. Is this the correct rendering of this verse from the original language? Well…let's take a look. Listed below are a few examples of how this verse should be translated.

Matthew 18:9 (Weymouth New Testament):

⁹And if your eye is causing you to fall into sin, tear it out and away with it; it is better for you to enter into Life with only one eye, than to remain in possession of two eyes but be thrown into the **Gehenna** of fire.

Matthew 18:9 (Young's Literal Translation):

⁹And if thine eye doth cause thee to stumble, pluck it out and cast from thee; it is good for thee one-eyed to enter into the life, rather than having two eyes to be cast to the **gehenna** of the fire.

Matthew 18:9 (The Emphasized Bible):

⁹And, if, thine eye, causeth thee to stumble, pluck it out, and cast it from thee: It is, seemly, for thee, one-eyed, into life, to enter, rather than, having two eyes, to be cast into the fiery **gehenna**.

Matthew 18:9 (The Concordant Version):

⁹And if your eye is snaring you, wrench it out and cast it from you. Is it ideal for you to be entering into life one-eyed, or, having two eyes, to be cast into the **Gehenna** of fire?

According to J. W. Hanson:

"**Gehenna**" was a well-known locality near Jerusalem, and ought no more to be translated "**hell**", than should Sodom or Gomorrah. See Josh. 15:8; II Kings 17:10; II Chron. 28:3; Jer. 7:31, 32; 19:2.

"**Gehenna**" is never employed in the Old Testament to mean anything else than the place with which every Jew was familiar.

The word should have been left untranslated as it is in some versions, and it would not be misunderstood. It was not misunderstood by the Jews to whom Jesus addressed it. Walter Balfour well says: "What meaning would the Jews who were familiar with this word, and knew it to signify the "**Valley of Hinnom**", be likely to attach to it when they heard it used by our Lord? Would they, contrary to all former usage, transfer its meaning from a place with whose locality and history they had been familiar from their infancy, to a place of misery in another world? This conclusion is certainly inadmissible. By what rule of interpretation, then, can we arrive at the conclusion that this word means a place of misery and death?" -end quote- (The Bible Hell, J. W. Hanson)

In just a short amount of time (with a little bit of research and study) we have put to rest the idea that the words "**hell**" and "**fire**" were spoken together by Jesus or anyone else for that matter. The words in question are "**Gehenna**" and "**fire**". Since we have already covered the topic of "**Gehenna**" in a previous objection, we will not say much at this time, except to reiterate that Jesus used the *literal* "**Gehenna**" of His day to warn the Jews of their destruction in 70-73 A.D., and to be a *metaphor* for the purifying "**fire**" of God which purges the garbage (or wood, hay, and stubble - carnality) in our lives. Once again, the spiritual aspect of this "**fire**" most assuredly speaks of purification, which eventually leads to correction and a change into the image of God.

UNQUENCHABLE FIRE

According to Lloyd Ellefson:

"In Mark 9:43-44, Jesus states…"than having your two hands, to go into **Gehenna**, into the **unquenchable fire**, where their **worm does not die**, and **the fire is not quenched**." An "**unquenchable fire**" is not an eternal "**fire**"; **it is a "fire" which cannot be put out**. It will continue to burn until it has accomplished its purpose. This "**fire**" will do the work it was sent to do! Jer. 17:27 says that God will kindle a "**fire**" in the gates of Jerusalem which will devour the palaces and "**it shall not be quenched**". However, we know it is not burning in Jerusalem at the present time. It has done its work." -end quote- (Fire: Natural And Spiritual, Lloyd Ellefson)

According to Otis Skinner:

"*Unquenchable fire*. This term is thus used by Jeremiah - "But if you will not hearken unto me…then will I kindle a **fire** in the gates thereof, and it shall devour the palaces of Jerusalem, and **it shall not be quenched**." - (Jer. 17:27) Here we have the phrase - "*not be quenched*". But the "**fire**" to which it refers ceased to burn when the temple at Jerusalem was consumed. **The term, therefore, does not imply endless burning**.

Worm dies not. Isaiah thus uses this expression - "And they shall go forth and look upon the carcasses of the men that have transgressed against Me; for **their worm shall not die, neither shall their fire be quenched**; and they shall be an abhorring unto all flesh." - (Isa. 66:24) Here the prophet alludes to the "**worms**" which preyed upon the **dead carcasses** that were **left unburied in the "Valley of Hinnom"**, when Jerusalem was destroyed. Those "**worms**" were not more than any of our own day; and were said to die not, because "**worms**" were always preying there. **The expression, therefore, does not denote endless suffering**." -end quote- (The Doctrine Of Endless Misery Not Taught In The Bible, Otis Skinner)

As we can see, "**unquenchable fire**" (whether in the natural or the spiritual) does not denote *endless* "**fire**", but rather, it speaks of a "**fire**" which **CANNOT BE PUT OUT "UNTIL" IT HAS ACCOMPLISHED ITS PURPOSE!** This is the consuming "**fire**" of God. His "**fire**" is "**UNQUENCHABLE**". The next time you find yourself in the midst of a "**fiery**" trial, please understand that your trial is the very "**unquenchable fire**" of Almighty God. It cannot and will not be put out "until" it has served its purifying purpose. Thank God for His … "**UNQUENCHABLE FIRE**"!

THE LAKE OF FIRE

According to J. Preston Eby:

"In my study of the "**lake that burns with fire and brimstone**" I was very much helped and impressed by the understanding given by Charles Pridgeon and I would like to quote from his scholarly work on the subject of "**BRIMSTONE**". He says: "The **Lake of Fire and Brimstone** signifies a "**fire**" burning with "**brimstone**"; the word "**brimstone**" or "**sulphur**" defines the character of the "**fire**". The Greek word "THEION" translated "**brimstone**" is exactly the same word "THEION" which means "divine". "**Sulphur**" was sacred to the deity among the ancient Greeks; and was used to fumigate, to purify, and to cleanse and consecrate to the deity; for this purpose they burned it in their incense. In Homer's *Iliad* (16:228), one is spoken of as purifying a goblet with "**fire and brimstone**". The verb derived from "THEION" is "THEIOO", which means to hallow, to make divine, or to dedicate to a god (See Liddell and Scott *Greek-English Lexicon*, 1897 Edition). **To any Greek, or any trained in the Greek language, a "lake of fire and brimstone" would mean a "lake of divine purification"**. The idea of judgment need not be excluded. **Divine purification** and **divine**

consecration are the plain meaning in ancient Greek. In the ordinary explanation, this fundamental meaning of the word is entirely left out, and nothing but eternal torment is associated with it." -end of Charles Pridgeon quote-

Continuation of quote from J. Preston Eby:

"I realize that the above thoughts define the subject very briefly, but let us summarize the meanings thus: "BURN" means combustion; to change the form of. "**FIRE**" means heat and light. "BRIMSTONE" means divine. Putting these three together can we not see that "**the lake burning with fire and brimstone**" is, actually, **DIVINE HEAT AND LIGHT PRODUCING A CHANGE!** Is such a process *eternal*? All the laws of nature shout that it is not! More than 2,500 years ago the Holy Spirit warned the wicked inhabitants of Jerusalem that God would kindle a fire at Jerusalem's gates which would devour her palaces. "But if you will not hearken unto Me...then will I kindle a "**fire**" in the gates thereof, and it shall devour the palaces of Jerusalem, and it shall "*not be quenched*" (Jer. 17:27). Did not God say this "**fire shall NOT BE QUENCHED?**" This prophecy was fulfilled and the fire did occur a few years later and it did destroy all the houses of Jerusalem (Jer. 52:13). Since God said no person or thing would "**quench this fire**", did that mean that it would *burn for ever*? Since it accomplished the work it was sent to do, and since it is NOT BURNING TODAY, it obviously went out *by itself* after accomplishing its purpose! **"Unquenchable fire" is not eternal fire - it is simply "fire" that cannot be put out until it has consumed or changed everything it is possible for it to change! It then simply goes out, for there is nothing more to burn.** Yet I hear the preachers ranting and raving about poor souls being cast into "**hell fire**" where "**their worm dies not, and the fire is not quenched**" and this, we are told, means eternal, unending torment. How foolish, illogical, and *deceptive*! Such a view contradicts the plain meaning of the term "**unquenchable**" and its use in the Word of God.

Suppose a few filthy, vile men and a few immoral women from some house of prostitution were *forced to sit* in the midst of a large congregation of singing, shouting, worshipping saints. *This certainly would be torment to most of them*. They would be tortured in the "**flames**" of the blazing glory of God in that place! If they were not held in their seats *by force*, most of them would rush out of there. I have been in meetings where I witnessed three responses to the glorious manifestation of the Lord's presence. First, the saints who loved the Lord rejoiced and adoringly worshipped. Some who were not Christians, but whose hearts were tender toward the Lord, came under deep conviction and, weeping and broken, gave themselves into the loving hands of Jesus. But others, filled with self, haters of righteousness, I have seen jump up and literally *run* out of a meeting - **TORMENTED IN THE PRESENCE OF THE LAMB**! Sure, they would rush, even run to get away from the convicting power of the Holy Ghost! I have seen it, and so have you. **To the unsaved, HIS GLORY is a "LAKE OF FIRE AND BRIMSTONE" - divine, cleansing, purging, purifying, consuming "fire"**! In ages yet unborn God shall expose ALL MEN to the sweet abiding presence of the Lamb. They will come under such severe processings, under such profound conviction that they will be tormented and have no rest day or night until they finally yield. And when they do, many fountains of tears will flow with weeping, praying, and calling upon the Lord." -end quote- (The Lake Of Fire, J. Preston Eby)

As we can see, the words **"lake of fire and brimstone"** mean: **DIVINE PURIFICATION**! Daniel saw it as a stream and John saw it as a lake. Can we now see that the words **"lake of fire and brimstone"** are to be understood symbolically, portraying a **"spiritual fire"** that is by nature corrective, and for the purpose of purification? This **"lake of fire"** speaks of God Himself and His ministers, for our **"God IS a consuming fire"**, making **"His ministers a flaming fire"** (Hebrews 12:29 and Psalm 104:4).

This experience of purification is to be for a period of time. IT IS NOT FOREVER! This can be discovered by studying the words **"olam"**, **"aion"**, and **"aionios"**, which words do show that God's judgments are **"of the ages"**, but not to continue past the ages, for the ages shall come to an end, and God shall be ALL IN ALL! <u>**OUR GOD IS A CONSUMING FIRE**</u>**! THANK GOD FOR HIS GLORIOUS LAKE OF FIRE!**

<u>Ladies And Gentlemen Of The Jury</u>…It has been brought to your attention in an undeniable fashion how that the terms **"hell fire"**, **"unquenchable fire"**, and **"lake of fire"** have been misunderstood by many to represent a literal fire for the purpose of eternal torture. This interpretation of **"fire"** misses the mark of the character and nature of God along with its true meaning of **pur**ification. Remember…These terms are all from the same Greek word #4442, **"pur"**. It is without a doubt that **"fire"** (in these instances) is for the purpose of **pur**ging, **pur**ifying, cleansing, and has a redemptive quality. Let us not forget that we are baptized in the Holy Ghost and **"fire"**; God is a consuming **"fire"**; we go through **"fiery"** trials; God makes His ministers a **"flaming fire"**, and Paul spoke of some believers being saved by **"fire"** (1st Corinthians 3:15). **"Fire"** is

actually our friend and is good for us. All must go through the "**fire**". Even Jesus was excited about "**fire**" in His day and wished all men were already going through the process, when He stated…"I have come to bring "**fire**" on the earth, and how I wish it were already kindled!" (Luke 12:49 New International Version)

OBJECTION #7 / WRATH, TORMENT, VENGEANCE, DESTRUCTION, JUDGMENT, & PUNISHMENT

1st John 4:8 declares that GOD IS LOVE! This gives us the very explanation of God - His essence, character, and nature. It actually defines Him in three words. It is not that God merely has love, or that He is just loving (or loves), but He IS love. The word "love" (that God IS) comes from the Greek word "agape" and is meant to portray UNCONDITIONAL LOVE. This type of love is unconditional, all giving, and always seeks to do what is best for the recipient, never expecting anything in return. "Agape" (God) cannot fail, will not fail, and never fails! Just read 1st Corinthians chapter thirteen. God's love (character and nature) has never failed, does not fail, and will never fail (whether now or in the ages to come) to reach every individual who has ever been born. Man and his poor puny *will* (limited ability under God's sovereignty to make choices) is and will be no match for the ferocious (extremely intense) love of Almighty God! All will bend the knee! All will confess with their lips! All will know Him…from the least to the greatest! Why…? **Because God is love, and love never fails! Be sure to let this soak in for a minute. LOVE (GOD) NEVER FAILS…NEVER…AT ANY TIME!**

Having said all of this, how then are we to understand "**wrath**", "**torment**", "**vengeance**", "**destruction**", "**judgment**" (also rendered as "**damnation**" in certain spots), and "**punishment**"? Well…there is only one possible way to understand these terms, and it is this: These extreme attributes that flow out of God's love are examples of his ***red hot and passionate love***, and are designed to bring forth correction, restoration, and reconciliation at all cost. These attributes do not define God, but they flow out of Who He IS. For example, while it is true that God will administer **wrath**, it would not be right to say that God *is* **wrath**. And this also holds true for the other attributes mentioned. Remember… God IS love! Out of His love flows "**wrath**", "**torment**", "**vengeance**", "**destruction**", "**judgment**", and "**punishment**". Once again, these attributes that flow out of His love are for the purpose of correction, restoration, and reconciliation at all cost, and they are limited in their duration ("aionios" - of the ages). Let us now delve into each of these attributes, for the Scriptures confirm and support the statements that have been made.

WRATH

According to Elwin Roach:

"The English word "**wrath**" comes from the Greek word "*orge*" (pronounced...or-gay). Strong's Exhaustive Concordance tells us that "***ORGE***" means: *desire, (as a reaching forth or excitement of the mind), i.e. (by analogy) violent passion*...If we follow the word to its derivatives we find that *it is akin to "**airo**", which implies a deliverance from sin, and is comparable to "**ornis**", which means "a bird" (as rising in the air). "Orge" is active. "Orge" reaches out and accomplishes its burning desire.* The passion *("**orge**" / "**wrath**")* we see in the Scriptures is usually in the context of heated determination. "**Wrath**" in the Biblical sense is not a condition of rage, as the word implies in the English, but is generally associated with adamant punishment toward those in rebellion; yet it does not end with punishment alone. We see that it ends in deliverance, especially at the judgment of the Last Death, the Lake of Fire. The passion of Christ, the "**wrath**" of the Lamb, is no doubt grievous to the carnal man, for it means the end of his lustful, self-indulging life. It is similar to a father's "**wrath**" when he punishes his rebellious son. It is not enjoyable to either of the two; yet it is done with understanding and in love, knowing the pain is but for a season and very necessary for the spirit of rebellion to be broken. This is in all of God's judgments toward His fallen creation." -end quote- (<u>Hell & The Lake Of Fire</u>, Elwin R. Roach)

It is now plain to see what is meant by the "**WRATH**" OF GOD. IT IS THE VERY PASSIONATE LOVE OF OUR FATHER! In essence, this love says...I LOVE YOU TOO MUCH TO LEAVE YOU IN YOUR CONDITION! I WILL <u>CORRECT YOU</u> BECAUSE I LOVE YOU!

As was stated earlier, "**wrath**" is the passionate love of God. It is His stored up desire and passion to see all of His creation set free. This is to be understood in the same sense of a man's passionate love for his bride. How would he react if his bride were to be wooed into the arms of another lover? He would go after his unfaithful bride in order to win her back again. In essence, he would unleash his "**wrath**" upon his bride. This "**wrath**" would not be to destroy her, but rather to bring her back in union with her true love. The man would pour out his passionate love in an effort to gain back his lover. He would exhaust all necessary means to draw her into his loving arms. HE WOULD STOP AT NOTHING, UNTIL SHE COULD FINALLY SEE HIS UNCONDITIONAL AND UNFAILING LOVE! After being a witness to this, the bride would voluntarily return to her one and only love. HOW COULD SHE RESIST SUCH FORGIVENESS, PASSION, DETERMINATION, AND LOVE?

There is no doubt that the Bible speaks of the "**wrath**" of God. The GOOD NEWS is that there is a purpose for the *WINEPRESS OF THE FIERCENESS AND "**WRATH**" OF ALMIGHTY GOD!* It is for the purpose of <u>correction</u>! It is His…DETERMINED, PASSIONATE LOVE!

It is also interesting to note…that from the Greek word "**orge**" ("**wrath**"), we get our English word "**orgasm**". This ought to tell us that this term has to do with **passionate love**…would you think?

Another point of interest is how "**wrath**" is spoken of in the book of Revelation as being "**finished**" or "coming to an end". In Revelation 15:1 it speaks of…"the seven last plagues; for in them is **filled up** the **wrath** of God." The words "filled up" in this verse come from the Greek word "teleo" and mean to "end" or "finish". The Greek word "teleo" is the same word used when Jesus was on the cross and said (John 19:30)…It is **finished**! So…The "**wrath**" of God will be **finished** and **come to an end**. It is not eternal. Hallelujah! Praise God!

If all of this information was not enough to properly understand the "**wrath**" of God (its purpose, and that it will come to an end), Isaiah 57:16 is the icing on the cake. It states…"For I will not contend forever, neither will I be always "**wroth**" (Old Testament word for "**wrath**"): for the spirit should fail before Me, and the souls which I have made." As a matter of fact, the next few verses after this speak of healing, restoration, and comfort. God is here telling us that His "**wroth**" ("**wrath**") is so powerful that the spirit and soul of man could not handle it forever. It says…the spirit and soul would fail (be overwhelmed). No one would be able to handle *eternal* "**wrath**". The very thought of it is ridiculous!

In no way are we attempting to paint a picture of God's "**wrath**" as though it will be a *picnic in the park*. But you can rest assured that "**wrath**" (as extreme as it may be) is God's determined and passionate love that will not let the sinner go and will result in all coming to the saving knowledge of the blood of the cross of Christ…Amen!

TORMENT

Revelation 14:10 states…"and he shall be **tormented with fire and brimstone** in the presence of the holy angels, and in the presence of the Lamb."

This is quite an interesting Scripture. Let us look at some of the key words in this verse and their meanings. The words "**fire and brimstone**" clearly speak of **DIVINE PURIFICATION**. This "**fire**" (which is a spiritual "**fire**") is the "**fire**" of God Himself. Its purpose is to consume wood, hay, and stubble (the carnality in man). Remember…GOD IS A CONSUMING "**FIRE**"!

According to Louis Abbott:

"There is an interesting rock used in Biblical days to test the quality of precious metals called a "**touchstone**". It is quite unfortunate that most translations following the King James tradition have hidden the Biblical references to this stone from us. The King James Bible Concordances have also hidden its meaning. Using the Strong's or Young's Concordances, when looking up the English word "**torment**", we discover that the noun for one of these Greek words is **basanoj** "**basanos**", Strong's number 931. Strong's number 928 "**torture**", and 929 "**torment**" are derivatives of this noun, "**basanos**", which Strong's Concordance says is a "**touchstone**". Webster's Collegiate Dictionary 5th Edition, tells us that a "**touchstone**" is "1. A black siliceous stone allied to flint; - used to test the purity of gold and silver by the streak left on the stone when rubbed by the metal. 2. Any test or criterion by which to try a thing's quality." Those of us who dig deep enough will discover why the early believers did not see the "**lake of fire**" as a place of "*eternal* **torment**". They knew that the wording in this passage referred to a place of **divine testing** and not a place of "*eternal* **torment**". The Greek word for "**sulfur**" is *qeiou* "theeion" which is akin to "theos", which means god. "**Sulfur**" ("**brimstone**") was used to purify temples in ancient days. It was also used for healing purposes. The fact that this passage of Scripture speaks of "day and night" proves that "aionas ton aionon" in this passage should not have been translated "forever and ever". Divine "**fire**" will test the works of men and angels." -end quote- (An Analytical Study Of Words, Louis Abbott)

We are now able to see that the word "**torment**" means *testing*. (A stone used to test the purity of gold.) Remember…Gold is symbolic of divinity, or that which is divine (God-like). The words "**tormented**" and "**lake of fire and brimstone**" clearly speak of a severe time of testing. This testing is for the purpose of purifying the person. The goal of God is to burn up the carnal nature in man, bringing him to the place where he is possessed by the divine nature. Notice where the testing is taking place…IN THE PRESENCE OF THE LAMB! THE VERY PRESENCE OF GOD IS A PURIFYING "**LAKE OF FIRE**"! This "**torment**" (severe testing), although severe, is not to "**torture**" the person forever, but rather, it is to correct, purify, and restore the person. It is to bring him to the place where he can embrace…THE PRESENCE OF THE LAMB!

VENGEANCE

Romans 12:19 states…"Dearly beloved, avenge not yourselves, but rather give place unto **wrath**: for it is written, **Vengeance** is Mine; I will repay, says the Lord." Sounds pretty bad, doesn't it? All "**judgment**", "**punishment**", "**wrath**", "**fire**", and "**vengeance**" Scriptures sound bad to the carnal mind. When we think of these terms, we think of God inflicting punishment, pain, injury, suffering, and loss for the purpose of vindication, satisfaction, and malicious retaliation. THIS TYPE OF THINKING IS NOT CORRECT! THIS IS THE WAY THAT THE CARNAL MIND PERCEIVES GOD AND HIS DEALINGS WITH MAN. COME OUT from this Babylonian mindset that paints a picture of God as an angry torture-hungry monster. GOD IS OUR FATHER! HE LOVES US! THAT IS WHY "**VENGEANCE**" BELONGS ONLY UNTO HIM! HE IS THE ONLY ONE WHO KNOWS HOW TO ADMINISTER IT IN A JUST WAY! If "**vengeance**" was left up to man, we would all be in BIG TROUBLE. We are mean, vindictive, malicious, and always on the lookout for retaliation. God, Who is our Father, is not like that.

According to Ray Prinzing:

"The word "**vengeance**" literally speaks of that action which is out of righteousness, out of that which is just, and for the purpose of bringing everything else into alignment with that which is just. Only a just action can produce justice. Two wrongs never make a right." -end quote- (<u>Redemption</u>, Ray Prinzing)

"**VENGEANCE**" IS A GOOD THING! IT IS A VERY GOOD THING! Only God has the power, wisdom, and love to bring it about in a just way. The Lord, through the manifested sons of God, shall declare the DAY OF THE "**VENGEANCE**" OF OUR GOD; to comfort all that mourn (Isaiah 61:2). Our God, Who is just, will not fail to repay every wrong, and to reward every right, while at the same time correcting, chastening, and restoring ALL THINGS AND ALL PEOPLE UNTO HIMSELF! VENGEANCE IS HIS…THANK GOD!

DESTRUCTION

1st Corinthians 3:17 states…"If any man defile the temple of God, him shall God **destroy**; for the temple of God is holy, which temple you are." The word "**destroy**" means: to waste, ruin, shrivel, wither, defile, to reduce a thing to useless fragments, and to extinguish. Now let us seek to understand what is meant when the Bible speaks of "**destruction**", for the real question is, what is it that is going to be "**destroyed**" (as far as man is concerned)?

You must put on the mind of Christ to be able to grasp Bible terminology. The "**destruction**" that is going to take place in man is to be understood in a spiritual sense. Here is a quote from *S. Ambrose of Milan* (390 A.D.) concerning the topic of "**destruction**".

"What then, hinders our believing that he who is beaten small as the **dust is not annihilated**, BUT IS CHANGED FOR THE BETTER: so that instead of an earthy man, he is made a spiritual man, and our believing that he who is "**destroyed**", is so "**destroyed**" that ALL TAINT IS REMOVED, and there remains what is pure and clean." -end quote-

This topic of "**destruction**" is further clarified in 1st Corinthians 5:5, that states…"to deliver such a one unto Satan FOR THE **DESTRUCTION** OF THE FLESH, THAT THE SPIRIT MAY BE SAVED IN THE DAY OF THE LORD."

Now we can see that God wants our flesh (carnality) to be "**destroyed**". That which is to be "**destroyed**" is NOT THE PERSON, but the flesh, the carnal mind, and the sin nature which separates us from the knowledge of God. God "**destroys**" the propensity within the sinner to sin, but He does not "**destroy**" the person himself. He "**destroys**" the wickedness in the wicked person, which in turn destroys the wicked. You could also say that God "**destroys**" the desire of the wicked, which in turn "**destroys**" His enemies, not that they cease to exist, BUT THAT THEY CEASE TO BE HIS ENEMIES!!!

So what is the result of the "**destruction**" of the flesh? The result is THAT THE SPIRIT WILL BE SAVED IN THE DAY OF THE LORD! HALLELUJAH!

We must ALL have the man of sin in us "**DESTROYED**" by the brightness of His coming (presence). God must "**destroy**", burn up, and consume the wood, hay, and stubble within man. This causes the gold, silver, and precious stones of the Spirit of God to be PURIFIED within us, making us partakers of the divine nature. Thank God for the…DESTRUCTION OF THE FLESH!

JUDGMENT

According to Ray Prinzing:

"Man has long viewed God's "**judgments**" as a vindictive action prompted by a motive for revenge and supported by a tumultuous "**wrath**" that must be pacified. NOT SO! Such is a gross caricature of our God! His mercy and grace are superabundant, and though He finds it necessary to chasten, His wisdom and righteousness produce a just and pure chastisement conditioned to correct the situation, and thus bring forth a creature improved by the process." -end quote- (Redemption, Ray Prinzing)

We must understand that all of God's "**judgments**" ARE CORRECTIVE IN NATURE! Hear it again! GOD'S "JUDGMENTS" ARE FOR THE PURPOSE OF CORRECTION! Jeremiah 10:24 states…"O Lord, CORRECT ME, BUT WITH **JUDGMENT**; not in Your anger, lest You bring me to nothing (lest You diminish me)." As you can see, "**judgment**" brings about correction, and correction is the result of "**judgment**". They go hand in hand. The Hebrew word for correct is "yasar", and has also been translated as - to instruct, to chasten, be taught, and be reformed. The Greek word is "paideuo", and includes the thought of child-training, involving the whole process of discipline which girds us up to the right way.

The purpose of God's "**judgments**", which are corrective, must always be seen in this light. If they were corrective in the past, and are corrective now, then they will be corrective in the ages to come. Remember…When God's "**judgments**" are in the earth, **the inhabitants of the world will learn righteousness** (Isaiah 26:9). Read 1st Chronicles 16:13-36 and Psalm 72. These passages of Scripture declare that the whole creation is longing for the "**judgment**" of God. Let the heavens be glad, and let the earth rejoice: and let men say among the nations, the Lord reigns! HIS "**JUDGMENTS**" ARE IN ALL THE EARTH!

PUNISHMENT

The following is a quote from A. P. Adams addressing the Greek word "kolasis" that was translated as "punishment" in Matthew 25:46 (KJV).

According to A. P. Adams:

"The purpose of "**punishment**" is not only the protection of society, and the restraint of the offender, but also his reformation; this latter should be the main purpose of "**punishment**"; any "**punishment**" that is not conducive to this end is wholly unjustifiable, it is simply an attempt to overcome one evil with a greater evil; - **now to talk about endless "punishment", is nonsense, as much as it would be to talk of endless correction, or endless reforming.** You might speak of endless torture, or endless suffering; but *endless* "**punishment**" is not a proper collection of terms at all. I will add that the original word here rendered "**punishment**" signifies a "**punishment**" for the correction and bettering of the individual, hence it could not be *endless*." -end quote- (Definitions: Eternal, A. P. Adams)

Notice how this verse reads from The New Testament In Modern Speech. It reads as follows…"And these shall go away into **the Punishment of the Ages**, but the righteous into **the Life of the Ages**." (Matthew 25:46, Weymouth New Testament)

What is being discussed here is *"punishment"* and *life* within the ages of time (of or belonging to the ages). As we know, the Bible teaches the ages will come to an end. Since "**punishment**" ("kolasis") signifies a "**punishment**" for the correction and bettering of the individual, it is *impossible* for it to be *endless*. This is a sure word of interpretation due to the **double witness** within the same verse (that **"aionios"** refers to something **belonging to the ages of time**, and that **"kolasis"** most definitely refers to **correction, which by nature cannot be** *endless*). The key is in knowing that **God's "punishment" is for the purpose of correction**, which will naturally mean that when the offender (or nation) is corrected they will be restored to God. The ages were created by God for man to experience Him and to go through changes during this process. "**Punishment**" is one of those experiences that takes place during the ages and belongs to the ages. This is why it is always used in conjunction with the Greek word "aionios" (of or belonging to the ages).

Ladies And Gentlemen Of The Jury…We have been extremely careful and diligent (in painstaking fashion) to show that even the most extreme attributes of God (such as "**wrath**", "**torment**", "**vengeance**", "**destruction**", "**judgment**", and "**punishment**") flow out of the love of God and are for the purpose of **_correction_**! What else can be said, except to rejoice in the fact that our God's love and power shall be displayed in an unlimited fashion, and shall be demonstrated in such a way as to make even the most wicked of the wicked ultimately melt in the presence of the Lamb, embracing the inescapable love of God!

OBJECTION #8 / FEW THERE BE THAT FIND IT

Matthew 7:13-14 states…"Enter in at the strait gate: for wide is the gate, and broad is the way, that leads to destruction, and many there be which go in thereat: Because strait is the gait, and **narrow is the way**, which leads unto life, and **few there be that find it**." We have just quoted one of the most popular verses in the Bible. Now…Let us talk about what it means. Let us rightly divide this all-important passage of Scripture.

This passage of Scripture refers to the "**REMNANT**" (**the "overcomers", the "firstfruits company", the "body of Christ", the "barley company"**). It would do us well to remember, and to take note of, that there are Scriptures that refer to:

1. OVERCOMERS

2. THE CHURCH IN GENERAL

3. UNBELIEVERS

This happens to be a passage that talks about the "**overcomers**" ("**the few there be that find life**" in this present age). The subject matter of this passage is not, "flying off to heaven, or busting hell wide open after you die." As a matter of fact, Jesus spent very little time talking about what happens to man after physical death. His subject matter was always pertaining to THE KINGDOM OF GOD, WHICH HE DID SPEAK OF AS A PRESENT DAY REALITY, WAITING TO BE EXPERIENCED BY THOSE WHO WERE HUNGRY FOR GOD. Remember…The Kingdom of God is not a physical location that we are going to fly away to in the sweet by-and-by, but is defined as:

1. RIGHTEOUSNESS

2. PEACE

3. JOY…IN THE HOLY SPIRIT

This means that there are "**few**" who understand the Kingdom of God in this present age. There are "**few**" who SEE (PERCEIVE) the Kingdom of God. There are "**few**" who enter into this "**narrow way**" of the life of Christ, WHICH ENTAILS HAVING YOUR FLESH (YOUR CORRUPT NATURE, CARNAL MIND, WOOD, HAY, AND STUBBLE) DEALT WITH BY THE CONSUMING "**FIRE**" OF GOD! YES…IT IS A "**NARROW WAY**", AND "**FEW THERE BE THAT FIND IT**"!

There is only a "**remnant**" of people being dealt with in this present age, but the GOOD NEWS is, that **there are at least two more ages to come**, which will include the gathering in of THE CHURCH IN GENERAL AND THE UNBELIEVERS! (Read Ephesians 2:7.) Those who do not enter into this "**narrow way**" now are headed for destruction (loss / ruin).

Those who are in "**the narrow way now**" have already entered the PROCESS of the "**destruction of the flesh**". In essence, the "**destruction of the flesh**" is a good thing. With that being said though, IT IS BETTER to enter into the "**narrow way**" NOW, than having to suffer loss, being saved; yet so as by "**fire**" (1st Corinthians 3:15). As well, the unbeliever must go through the purifying "**fire**" of God, for our Father will leave nothing undone. For those who have the ears to hear, the Spirit calls for you to come into the "**narrow way**" of the Lord Jesus Christ NOW! But let us rest assured that ALL WILL EVENTUALLY COME TO THE FATHER, FOR JESUS ASSURED US THAT HE WOULD **DRAW (DRAG)** ALL MEN UNTO HIMSELF! PRAISE GOD FOR THE "**NARROW WAY**"!

The Barley Harvest ("**few there be that find it**") represents the first part of God's harvest. Those in this first harvest are referred to in Scripture as "overcomers". The gathering in of the **nations** is actually a *result* of the Barley Harvest. It is in and through the manifestation of the sons of God that all nations will come to know the Lord and serve Him. These "overcomers" shall come forth in the first resurrection to rule and reign on the earth under the leadership of the Lord Jesus Christ!

The Wheat Harvest represents "the church in general". It speaks of those who were justified by faith, but either did not go through or submit to the sanctification process of the Lord. They are believers, but are in need of further correction in order to be fully sanctified and put on the divine nature and character of their Heavenly Father. There still remains **iniquity (lawlessness)** in their lives that must be purged by the fire (the fiery law) of God. Those who are part of the Wheat Harvest shall be brought forth in the second resurrection to be saved *"yet so as through fire"* (1 Cor. 3:15).

The Grape Harvest represents "the unbelievers". It speaks of those who have neither been justified nor sanctified. They shall go through God's wrath, judgment, and the lake of fire for the purpose of correction.

The Good News to be associated with all of this is that these three harvests represent and guarantee the salvation of all in the fullness of time. As far as God is concerned, salvation for all is not "if", but "when". Let us call to remembrance what Paul told us in 1st Corinthians 15:22-23, which states…

[22]For as in Adam all die, so also in Christ all shall be made alive. [23]But each in his own order [tagma, "squadron"].

Here are some excerpts and quotes from the writings of Dr. Stephen Jones to support the things which have been stated. The quotes were taken from his writings entitled "Creation's Jubilee" and "The Restoration Of All Things". They are from various spots throughout these written works.

According to Dr. Stephen Jones:

"If we were to study the passages in the Bible where barley is mentioned, we would find much valuable information about the first resurrection and the character and calling of those who qualify for it. The fact that barley matures early tells us that the "barley firstfruits" are the first people to mature spiritually to bring forth the fruits of the kingdom that God requires. Barley also can survive drought, heat, and cold much more easily than can wheat.

The Church in general will be raised in the second resurrection. Jesus calls them "the just" who receive Life at the same time "the unjust" are judged at the beginning of that final age in the lake of fire. In either case, the fire that judges is the same fire poured out on Pentecost. God's judgment is designed to *"thoroughly clear His threshing floor; and He will gather His wheat into the barn"* (Matthew 3:12).

The baptism of fire upon the wheat (Church) is both good and bad. It represents a purification process, which is judgment upon sin in order to bless the individual. When God works to refine or purify someone, it is not a pleasant experience. No judgment is. But those who understand the mind and purpose of God will readily submit to

His fire, knowing that God is working all things out for their good.

Finally, a Biblical study of the grape harvest, with the treading of the grapes in the winepresses, tells us the fate of the unbelievers. The winepress depicts God's wrath, judgment, and the lake of fire.

The purpose of the grain harvests of spring (barley and wheat) is to provide bread for God's great communion table. The purpose of the Feast of Tabernacles with its celebration of the winepress is to provide the wine for God's table. Without this wine, His communion table would have only bread and would be incomplete. God will have His wine, but it must come by means of the winepress, which speaks of the judgments of God.

God harvests His barley, wheat, and grapes in different manners, even as nature teaches us. The chaff from the barley falls away very easily, so barley is said to be *winnowed*. That is, the action of the wind itself (by means of fans) are sufficient to get rid of the chaff. This speaks of the barley company, who so quickly respond to the wind of the Spirit.

To remove the chaff from the wheat requires threshing. This is a more severe action, but it does the job. It depicts the fact that the Church will be harvested by means of judgment, or tribulation. The Latin word, *tribulum*, is a threshing instrument.

Finally, to obtain the juice the grapes must be trodden under foot. Grapes do not have chaff, but they do have "flesh" that must be pressed severely in order to obtain the wine. This represents the most severe form of judgment upon the unbelievers. Yet the result is that God obtains wine for His communion table." -end quote- (Creation's Jubilee, Dr. Stephen Jones)

According to Dr. Stephen Jones:

"There is more than one resurrection coming. The first "squadron" will be those who are called to rule and reign with Him (Rev. 20:4-6). The second group will be those believers who are raised along with all the unbelievers (John 5:28, 29; Luke 12:46) at the Great White Throne (Rev. 20:11-13). This second group of believers will miss the first resurrection and will not reign with Christ during the thousand years in the Tabernacles Age to come. Nonetheless, they will certainly be *"saved yet so as through fire"* (1 Cor. 3:15). Jesus made it clear in Luke 12:46-49 that those servants of God who mistreated others would receive a "flogging" before being given their reward.

The third group will be the unbelievers themselves, after their time of judgment has been completed, for there will be a Jubilee at the end of time according to the law, wherein all of creation will be set free in the glorious liberty of the children of God (Rom. 8:21)." -end quote-(<u>The Restoration Of All Things</u>, Dr. Stephen Jones)

<u>Ladies And Gentlemen Of The Jury</u>…There is no false teaching that cannot be exposed by simply rightly dividing the Word of God. If we say…"**few there be that find it**" refers to only some being saved as opposed to the rest being lost forever, that is just not Scripturally correct. As we apply ourselves to understand the Feasts of the Lord we will see that God's three harvests of souls will include all in the fullness of time - **"overcomers", "the church in general", and "unbelievers"**.

OBJECTION #9 / *FREE WILL*

Since this article is about the balanced view of God's *sovereignty* and man's *authority*, it is at this time we will discuss *authority* in relation to the term and *so-called* belief of *"free will"* and offer some concluding remarks. Here are a few words from Dr. Stephen Jones from his article entitled, "How To Believe In God's Sovereignty Without Being A Fatalist"…

"Man's *authority* is NOT the same as "**free will**", although many have confused the two and have tried to prove "**free will**" by pointing to Scriptures that establish man's *authority*. Only *sovereignty* has *"free will"*. *Authority* is limited.It is my hope and purpose to bring people to a closer balance in understanding how God's *sovereignty* and man's *authority* operate at the same time. This, in turn, could help resolve some of the long-standing doctrinal disputes between the two sides, as well as help people get a clearer perspective of God's ability to accomplish His purposes for the earth - and for each person as an individual…

"The quick answer is that *man's authority ends where God's sovereignty begins*. Man has the *authority* to reject God **for a time**, but ultimately, God's *sovereign will* is going to be fulfilled. Man can reject God and receive judgment, but God's judgment itself will correct his fleshly disposition so that he genuinely submits to Jesus Christ…

"We have shown this in other writings, summarized best in the short booklet, If God Could Save Everyone - Would He? There we show that man has *authority* over his own "land" that God has given him as his inheritance; but God yet retains *sovereignty* over him by right of creation.

The *authority* that God has given man is limited. Man does not have the ability to sell himself to the devil (or to the flesh) for ever. He can do so only within the parameters of time." -end quote- (How To Believe In God's Sovereignty Without Being A Fatalist, Dr. Stephen Jones)

For example, let us consider the story of Jonah...

God tells Jonah to go to Nineveh and cry against it for its wickedness. Jonah rose up to flee unto Tarshish from the presence of the Lord. He found a ship going to Tarshish, paid the fare, and ran from the presence of the Lord (so he thought). In simple terms, God asked Jonah to do something, and Jonah said NO! He made a choice to disobey and reject God. Later in the story..."THE LORD SENT OUT A GREAT WIND INTO THE SEA, AND THERE WAS A MIGHTY TEMPEST IN THE SEA, SO THAT THE SHIP WAS LIKE TO BE BROKEN." (Jonah 1:4) In the midst of the storm Jonah asks the men on the ship to throw him overboard into the sea. So...they threw Jonah into the sea and the storm stopped. Not only this, but..."the Lord had prepared a *great fish to swallow up Jonah. And Jonah was in the belly of the fish three days and three nights."* (Jonah 1:17) How interesting to find out next...**_THEN JONAH PRAYED!!!_** *I wonder what it was that caused Jonah to pray??? Do you think it might have had something to do with that great big ol' fish that God had prepared for him???*

After God got done dealing with Jonah and asked him to go to Nineveh again...Jonah said..."*No problem Lord...I'm your man!*" **This time Jonah made a choice to obey the Lord.** *Do you think it might have had something to do with that storm and that great fish???* I think so!!!

Folks...This is really not that complicated. Jonah initially made a choice to run from the Lord, and then he made a choice to obey the Lord. BUT....in between all of this there was a storm and a *great big fish*! **If you were to take the *storm* and the *great fish* out of the equation, Jonah would not have obeyed the Lord!** So...what does all of this mean?

Yes...there are people who are running from the Lord now and who are headed to Tarshish (spiritually speaking). BUT...God has prepared a *storm* and a *great fish* for them down the line to *swallow them up* called..."*the lake of fire*" (God's storm and great fish for all of mankind). I can promise you this...When unbelievers find themselves in the "lake of fire"...**_THEN THEY WILL PRAY!!!_** It is no different than the story of Jonah. God will correct them and purify them that they will be able to submit to and believe on the Lord Jesus Christ for justification, sanctification, and glorification. He will ask them again (like in the case of Jonah)…BELIEVE ON THE LORD JESUS CHRIST…and they will say just like Jonah…"YES…I'm your man!"

It is not hard for God to cause adverse circumstances that will enable us to change our will and make the right choice. **We must stop making an idol out of the "will" of man.** It is not sovereign over God. Yes…we are able to make choices, but God in His sovereignty has the last say, and is able to show us what the right choice is to make. **He loves us too much** to leave us for *all eternity* in the consequences of a bad choice. He just will not let it happen! **Plus…WE ARE HIS PROPERTY, AND WE HAVE BEEN BOUGHT WITH A PRICE. HE IS GOING TO GET EVERYTHING HE PAID FOR - THE HUMAN RACE!**

In conclusion, the Biblical facts of the matter are simply this:

God is *sovereign*, but does not force and manipulate our every thought and action, even though He is able to do so. He does at times override our *will*, but not all the time because He wants to teach us how to receive, handle, and use *power*, *authority*, *responsibility*, *accountability*, *stewardship*, and *choices*. On the other hand, man has *authority* and a *will*, but both are limited. They are not unlimited and totally *"free"* and to be seen as *sovereign* over God. And THANK GOD that He has not given us an unlimited amount of *authority* and *"free will"* in our present state with which we would run the risk of consigning ourselves for ever to a lost condition. Remember…we are the property of God. He will not let this happen. God has the final say.

According to John Gavazzoni:

"**Now some, completely indoctrinated by the dumbed-down notion of "free will",** upon being confronted with what I've just shared, without any depth of thought at all, **would accuse me of making man out to be a mere robot.** But, I ask, if God has a *"free will"*, and brings man into participation with that will, how can freedom be defined as robotic? Freedom by definition, involves not being controlled by another. **The relationship of God's will to us, is not one of making us do something against our will, but by bringing our will into union with His. This is not coercion, this is causation,** and it is causation by the force of love which ultimately **worked by God leaving us to ourselves to do what we would do left to ourselves; which was to crucify His Son, and then to love such enemies back to Himself by the power of forgiving love."**
-end quote- (Free Will, John Gavazzoni)

<u>Ladies And Gentlemen Of The Jury</u>…It is as simple as that! This matter is not as complicated as many have made it out to be. God is in control of everything, but gives man an opportunity to experience a measure of His *power* and *authority* and how to use it in the proper way. Those who *pass the test* will be the ones to pull the King's Carriage (so to speak) and usher in the manifestation of the sons of God at the appointed time. They will then be a vessel of God's *authority* in the fullness and rule the nations, teaching them the righteousness of God until every knee bows to Jesus Christ and every tongue confesses Him as Lord of all to the glory of God the Father!

OBJECTION #10 / THE POWERS OF DARKNESS

Question:

Does the reconciliation of all things include the powers of darkness?

Answer:

YES…OF COURSE IT DOES! It is the reconciliation of ALL THINGS!

Colossians 1:16-20 is an incredible passage of Scripture that explains to us in great detail that there is to be a reconciliation of all things. This reconciliation of all things is a direct result of the cross of the Lord Jesus Christ. PRAISE GOD…That is a powerful cross! Thank God for the cross (the atonement) of the Lord Jesus Christ! Colossians 1:16-20 states… "**For by Him were all things created**, that are in heaven, and that are in earth, visible and invisible, whether they be **thrones, or dominions, or principalities, or powers: all things were created by Him, and for Him**: And He is before all things, and by Him all things consist. And He is the Head of the body, the church: Who is the beginning, the firstborn from the dead; that in all things He might have the preeminence. For it pleased the Father that in Him should all fullness dwell; And, **having made peace through the blood of His cross, by Him to reconcile all things unto Himself**; by Him, I say, whether they be things in earth, or things in heaven."

As well, Ephesians 3:9-11 sheds light on this subject. It states…"And to make all men see what is the fellowship of the mystery, which from the beginning of the world has been hid in **God, Who created all things by Jesus Christ**: To the intent that now unto **the principalities and powers in heavenly places might be known by the church the manifold wisdom of God**, According to the eternal purpose which He purposed in Christ Jesus our Lord."

Many people have no understanding at all that GOD IS SOVEREIGN, and that God is responsible for having created ALL THINGS, INCLUDING "**SATAN AND THE POWERS OF DARKNESS**". In our daily Christian walk we find ourselves fighting against principalities, powers, rulers of the darkness of this world, and spiritual wickedness in high places. Well…THE SCRIPTURES HAVE JUST TOLD US THAT GOD IS RESPONSIBLE FOR HAVING CREATED THESE "**FORCES OF DARKNESS**". "**Principalities and Powers**" are created and used by God, according to the eternal purpose (the purpose of the ages) which He purposed in Christ Jesus. They are used to shape and mold the sons and daughters of God into the very image of God. They are merely a tool in God's tool box. HOW CAN THIS BE?

In order for God to bring about His purpose of the ages there had to be **opposition** and obstacles for His children to overcome. God created "**the powers of darkness**" (including Satan - the prince of the power of the air - the spirit that now works in the children of disobedience), giving His children something to overcome. We must understand that God wanted overcomers. In order for there to be overcomers there had to be something to overcome. So…God made sure to it that there would be things to overcome. When the purpose of God is completed (at the end of the ages) there will be no more need for "**the powers of darkness**", at which time these powers, WHICH GOD CREATED…SHALL BE PUT BACK IN THE TOOL BOX AND RECONCILED (MADE FRIENDLY) UNTO HIM!

Ladies And Gentlemen Of The Jury…We will now turn our attention to the words of J. Preston Eby as we consider this topic of "**the powers of darkness**"…

According to J. Preston Eby:

"The message is clear - we now wrestle against wicked spirits, not only on earth, but in the heavenly sphere. That this conflict is real, none can deny. But what shall be the end of these wicked spirits, these principalities and powers in heavenly places? "Eternal torment in hell fire!" you say. That there is much "**hell**" and "**torment**" ahead for these wicked ones I have no doubt. But when the ages have run their course, when the Sons of God have finished their ministry of reconciliation, when all the purposes of God have been consummated, brought to expected end, what then? The testimony of God stands sure: "For by Him were **ALL THINGS created**, that are IN HEAVEN, and that are IN EARTH, visible and INVISIBLE, whether they be thrones, or dominions, or

PRINCIPALITIES, or POWERS: ALL THINGS were created by Him and FOR HIM: and, having made peace through the blood of His cross, by Him to **RECONCILE ALL THINGS unto Himself**; by Him, I say, whether they be THINGS IN EARTH, or THINGS IN HEAVEN" (Col. 1:16, 20).

You may say - "I do not believe it! I do not, I cannot believe that Jesus died to reconcile "**wicked, foul, hostile, filthy spirits**" in the heavenly realms unto God!" Tell it not to me, my brother, my sister, tell it to the Holy Spirit for it is He, and none other, who inspired those awesome words. All your letters of protestation addressed to me will be thrown in the trash, for I possess no power to change even one jot or tittle of Holy Writ. When God declares that **the blood of the cross of Jesus Christ avails to reconcile "principalities and powers" IN HEAVEN AND IN EARTH**, I have absolutely no ability to do anything about it. God will do what He says He will do whether or not you or I like it, and whether or not we believe it. Your unbelief will not make the grace and power of God of none effect. God will finish His UNIVERSAL RECONCILIATION either *through you…precious friend of mine…or in spite of you.*"-end quote- (Reconciliation In The Heavens, J. Preston Eby)

CONCLUSION

Many also reject the reconciliation of all things on the grounds that it diminishes the atonement or makes it worthless (so they say). They go on to ask the question…"If all will be saved, then why did Jesus die?" That, my friend, shows two things: We have not understood why Jesus died, and we have not understood that the reconciliation of all things in no way diminishes the atonement, but rather, it glorifies the blood of the cross of Christ much greater than the false teaching of eternal torture. First and foremost, Jesus died to save us from a condition (sin - the sin nature, which produces the carnal mind), not an after-death physical location. Second, which glorifies the cross of Christ more….some being saved, or ALL being saved? I think we can figure that one out with just a *smidge* of reasoning and meditation.

To ask…*why did Jesus die* in light of all being saved in the end, would be like asking a firefighter who knew he was able to go into a burning house and save all who were trapped…"Why go into the house if all will be saved." That is absurd…ridiculous. We know why…TO SAVE ALL WHO ARE IN THE HOUSE! Why did Jesus die then…well…TO SAVE ALL! HE DIED TO SAVE THE WORLD! ALL WILL BE SAVED

BECAUSE HE DIED! It is not rocket science folks! It is not a matter of *if*, but *when*. All will be awakened to have faith and believe on the Lord Jesus Christ, every man in his own order. Once these popular objections are brought to your attention, exposed for their inaccuracy, and dismantled by the Spirit and truth of the Scriptures, you will have no choice but to believe in the reconciliation of all things...BECAUSE IT IS THE TRUTH!

If all will not be saved in the end it can only bring us to two possible conclusions: God cannot save all, or God does not want to save all - He either can't or He won't. This would leave us with a God Who is either weak or cruel. As a son of the living God, I am here to tell you THAT OUR GOD IS NOT WEAK OR CRUEL...HE IS THE SAVIOR OF THE WORLD! **<u>PLEASE</u>** open up your heart to the things which have been unlocked to you in an undeniable and indisputable manner, through the avenues of **The Holy Scriptures**, **Word Meanings**, and **Revelation Truth**. May God give you the spirit of wisdom and revelation in the knowledge of Him!

PART 10 - THE MAN WITH THE BOOTS

The day was Wednesday, August 1, 2001. I was starting a new job with Acoustical Specialties in Baton Rouge, Louisiana. I had been out of work for about a month, after being laid off by Norandex Building Materials, which was also located in Baton Rouge. Norandex decided to shut down their Baton Rouge branch at that time for many and varied reasons. Prior to my start date of the new job, a friend of mine put in a good word for me with the owner of Acoustical Specialties. I sat down with the owner and he told me there would be an opening in the Brick Division. After talking with him, he gave me the opportunity to come to work for his company. The start date was set for Wednesday, August 1, 2001.

My new position was similar to what I had been doing at Norandex (selling vinyl siding and windows), but now I would just have to learn some new products, like: brick, insulation, fireplaces, and a few others. I can still remember my first day on the new job. Shortly after arriving I was introduced to an older gentleman by the name of **Louis Thompson**. He had a cup of *coffee* in his hand and he was wearing a pair of what he calls...*round toe work boots*. I had come to find out later that three of his four passions were his *boots, coffee, and college football*. We will talk about his fourth passion in a minute, but back to the *coffee, boots, and college football* for now. He would later tell me that his favorite *coffee* was *Community Coffee* (made by a Louisiana based *coffee* company founded by *Cap Saurage* in 1919). He was a "master" at making and drinking *coffee*. When he would go to make a *fresh pot of coffee*, he would try to put in just enough *coffee*, but not too much, in an effort to make *the perfect pot of coffee*. After it would brew and he tasted it, he would always let you know if he had *hit it right on or not*!

I would also come to learn that his *boots* were a big part of his work day, since he was always on his feet and on job sites measuring for brick and other building products. He definitely favored the *round toe work boot* as opposed to the *narrow toe cowboy boot*. He would always say how comfortable *his boots* were in comparison to *those cowboy boots* which would *squish your toes all up*.

Down the line it became obvious that he was a *die-hard college football* fan. We always spent time during football season analyzing the games together. To know **Louis Thompson**, was to see him with a cup of *coffee* in his hand, talking about *college football*, ready to take on the day, neatly dressed, and with <u>clean</u> *round toe work boots*.

Having said all that…back to my first day of work now…

My new boss told me he would be pairing me up with **Louis** in order to *learn the ropes* of this new position. This took place immediately. From day one we started riding and working together. He was the best one to teach me the job, for <u>he had been selling brick longer than I had been alive</u>. As we rode together and worked different job sites, it did not take me long to *crack up laughing* and pick up on his many *one-liners and jokes*, like:

"too much *sugar* for a *dime*"…"momma taught me to *live poor*"…"momma taught me….if what you are trying is not working…*my God*…please try something else"…"*life is easy*…we are the ones who make it hard"…"the *eagle* (our paycheck) has landed (he called it a *buzzard* on a bad week)"…"the *crape myrtle limb* is the cure for A.D.D. (Attention Deficit Disorder)"…"*riffy*"…"*shaky*"…"in Pumpkin Center (where he grew up)…the only *cents* we had was *common cents*"…"plain old *horse sense*"…"I'm not *readin'* what you're saying"…"*what?*………"… "*huh?*………"…"if I tell you *a hen dips snuff*…you can look under a wing and find a can"…"that's not *real* coffee"…"*well*…there's a little more to it"…"I don't believe *everything* that *anybody* says"…"go for the *gold*"…"a *bird in the hand*"…"bring it on *home*"…"the *Thursday Door* (the one we would leave out of after the *eagle* had landed)"…"*listen at em…listen at em*"…"whatever cranks your *tractor* or floats your *boat*"…"this is *gonna rattle your cage*"…"a *can't miss*"…"that *dog* won't hunt"…"I don't have a *dog* in this race"…"I can't *buy* that"…"this is not my *first rodeo*"…"I'm not lookin' for a *feather* in my hat"…"I'm too old to use a planner…I already know what I'm gonna do…as little as I can and as fast as I can"…and on and on…there are too many to name…it would *literally* take up an entire book!

Also (and most importantly), it took no time at all, even from the very first day, to learn of his fourth and most important passion - **GOD!** **Louis** wasted no time at all by beginning to tell his story to me of his journey with God over the years. One of the first stories he told me was of an encounter he had with his good friend **Norwood Smith**. **Louis** was always analyzing where he had been, where he was now, and where he was headed in God. He was just that way - an analyzer.

 One day he was at **Norwood's** house and he began to tell **Norwood** how he saw the condition of the world, the church, and the current generation of young people. **Louis** gave his side of the story and how he was looking for a "solution" to find his way out and back to God, bringing others with him who could hear the call. After hearing all of this, **Norwood** took a break from eating his *TV dinner*, *balled up* his napkin in the palm of his hand, and *dragged* it across his lips, saying…"I don't know what you're talkin' bout." **Louis** then told **Norwood**…"*Well*…I have got to go back, retrace my steps, find out what went wrong, and find my way back to God." As **Louis** was heading out the door, **Norwood** spoke up again and said…"Hey *Thomp* (short for **Thompson** and pronounced *tōmp* with a *long ō sound*)…ain't nobody goin' with *ya*…" Well…I took him up on the offer years later when I finally met him at Acoustical Specialties and took that trip back with him…**the whole trip!**

For the next **seven years and seven days** we worked together…side by side. We were inseparable! One person who constantly saw us together over the years began to call me **his shadow**. He would say…"Here comes **Louis** and **the shadow** again." What I learned during those **seven years and seven days** from "The Man With The Boots" has *turned over my apple cart (another one of his one-liners)* for all of time and beyond. So…*kick back…relax…and by all means…get a cup of coffee* (in honor of "The Man With The Boots")…"*Here we geaux Tigers, here we geaux!*" **(For those of you who are not aware:"Geaux" is a French word-play on the verb "go". It originated from areas highly populated with**

Cajun Americans, Louisiana State University Tiger Fans, or more commonly both.)

BURN OUT...FOR MANY MONTHS...AS PURE GOLD

One particular event that was very precious to **Louis**, and that he would refer to quite frequently, was a prophecy that was spoken over his life years before I had met him. The name of the man that prophesied over him was **Randy Bardwell** - a missionary to Honduras, but at the time, **Randy** was in the United States. **Louis** recalls (as he tells the story) that the way in which the prophecy was given was not with pomp and circumstance, and was not loud and boisterous. When **Randy** gave the prophecy (according to **Louis**) it was simple, soft spoken, and to the point. **Randy** prophesied by the Spirit of the Lord that **Louis**..."*would go through the fire for many months and burn out as pure gold.*" Whenever **Louis** speaks of this event he mentions how real it felt and how genuine he believes the prophecy was that night and still is.

PRAY FOR TRUTH

As **Louis** tells the story, the next way in which God dealt with him **(for approximately thirteen years)** was to "pray for truth". To know **Louis**, was to know him as a prayer warrior and faithful reader of the Scriptures. His usual custom was to wake at about 5:00 AM every morning and to read one chapter in the Old Testament and one chapter in the New Testament. He would also make a point every Monday morning to be to work at 6:00 AM for a weekly prayer meeting. During this time of prayer he did not come to pray for material things or for God to do things for him as most pray, but rather, "he prayed for truth" as God had put it on his heart to do so. As a matter of fact, HE PRAYED FOR TRUTH FOR THIRTEEN YEARS! Some of the workers at Acoustical Specialties would join him from time to time, and the number of those who attended actually got up to about half a dozen or so at one point. But they would always drop out after a while. It may have had something to do with 6:00 AM on a Monday, or so you would think.

No matter what happened, **Louis** remained faithful to what God had called him to do - "pray for truth"! After a while it had pretty much dwindled down to just **Louis** and one other person (**Nathan Selders**) who would come on Monday mornings to pray. **Louis** continued to "go for the *gold*" and believe God had called him to intercede and stand in the gap for his family, his friends, the pastors in the town of Baton Rouge, his company, and to "pray for truth". He could still hear the voice of God telling him…"pray for truth, Pray For Truth, PRAY FOR TRUTH!"

POSITION OF TESTIMONY

After having diligently prayed for "truth" for thirteen years, **Louis** came across a minister on the radio who began to give him the answer to his prayers. The Spirit of God spoke through this minister and his radio program, telling the listeners how they were to take a "position of testimony" while on the job, at the house, out in public, or wherever they were. This "position of testimony", which is our position IN CHRIST, made him free and set him on a journey in which he discovered all the things (truths) he had longed for in his time of diligent prayer before the Lord. Whenever **Louis** tells the story of how he received this knowledge, he will surely tell you how he rejoiced the day he heard it on the radio as he was driving on the interstate. It was so liberating to him that he would do a little *victory dance ("charismatic jig")* from time to time as he celebrated before the Lord. The Lord had given **Louis** the Scriptural prescription which would bring knowledge, victory, and power. He no longer went to work, thinking that any one person or situation was his problem. He knew he did not have to try and fight with anyone or anything that came his way. He simply took his "position of testimony" and let the Lord fight his battles. He was in position to be used of the Lord and open and ready to "HEAR" from the Lord.

THE MIRROR SERMON

Now that **Louis** knew to take his position of testimony, God had showed him just how simple his Christian walk really was. It was now just down to God and **Louis**. No need to *duke it out* with co-workers, family, friends, or situations. **Louis** always said…"Even if someone or something outside of you is causing you a problem…it is still YOUR problem." And with that being said, he would take HIS problem and bring it to God - between God and **Louis. He called all of this… "looking in the mirror / the mirror sermon".** He used to say…"When God first told me to look in the mirror (spiritually speaking) it was ugly. But as soon as I did…He was right there…He rushed in to comfort me and let me know it was going to be alright. He showed me who I was, Who He was, my problem, and His solution." **Louis** was well on his way now to apprehending what he had been after for so long - "truth" (and revelation truth at that…The Revelation Of Jesus Christ). What **Louis** was seeing is what we all need to see. It is what the apostle Paul talked about when he said…"For I know that in me (that is, in my flesh,) dwells no good thing: for to will is present with me; but how to perform that which is good I find not." (Romans 7:18) The *old man* was exposed to **Louis**, and he was now about to be ushered into the most *magnificent truth* contained within the pages of the Holy Scriptures. He was about to see just how powerful His God really was, and to know beyond a shadow of a doubt…WHO HE IS!

WHO HE IS

For as far back as **Louis** could remember, he always struggled with the idea (according to what most of those in Christianity teach) that God would lose the vast majority of the human race to an *eternal* hell. He used to tell me over and over again…"I just can't *buy* that." He would go on to say, asking questions like…"How could God take that big of a loss and still be God?...What happened to the fact that He is supposed to be all-loving and all-powerful?...How could Adam bring the whole creation down into sin and death, but Jesus Christ can only *get a few back* (so to speak)?...How can God be Wonderful, Counselor, The Mighty God, The Everlasting Father, and The Prince of Peace, and be defeated by the powers of darkness, the fall of Adam, and the will of man?" Once again he would say…"I just can't *buy* that…*that dog just won't hunt.*" **Louis** told me on many occasions that he went along with the *status quo* message of the church for years, but always questioned deep down in his heart many of the things that were taught.

This went on until one day…**Louis** came across a certain minister on the radio (while driving in his car) who was teaching that ultimately… all would be saved and restored in Jesus Christ. He also marveled at how well this minister handled his attackers who would call in to the show and *lambast him* for making such statements. The minister would simply say…"*My man…look here…here is how it is*"…and so on, explaining to them what they could not see, and remaining calm with his persecutors. This minister went on to teach **the reconciliation of all things through the blood of the cross of Christ**, exposing the false teaching of *eternal* hell, and in turn **Louis** found the answer he had been looking for his whole life - THAT GOD REALLY WAS THE SAVIOR OF THE WORLD! Now he was able to say with confidence…"I know WHO GOD IS!"

After **Louis** believed this for some time, it was brought to his attention (by his brother **"Root Beer"**) that his son (**Billy**) believed in an ultimate salvation of all men through Jesus Christ. The ironic part in all of this is that **Louis** and his son went through a season where they did not believe the same things concerning God, but they were now *on the same page*, united in truth by the Spirit of the Lord! **Louis** told his brother he had already received this revelation and believed the same thing. Shortly after that **Louis** and his son got together to drink some coffee and talk things over. When they sat down at the table together and began to talk it was as if they had believed these things all their life and were *on the same page* concerning God ultimately saving all men. They were speaking the same language, using the same terminology, and in agreement, being in one mind and one accord. What could have possibly caused this to happen? Well…You guessed it…***"EARS TO HEAR"!*** They had both tapped into "hearing what the Spirit is saying unto the churches". This makes all the difference in the world. They were the ones to first introduce me to this great truth. **I am so glad they did!**

So many times **Louis** would bring to my attention the fact that it was a "must" to know…WHO HE IS (speaking of God, of course). He would go on to say…**"Thomas**…The problem of the church is that they don't know WHO HE IS! When they know WHO HE IS, they will stop teaching things that do not line up with WHO HE IS!" He would always "equate" God's ability to bring everything back to Himself as **unlimited love and power**, and the way the church (by and large) taught God losing the vast majority of the human race as **loss and weakness**. After **Louis** saw the "WHO HE IS FACTOR" about God he was never the same again, **and neither will you be when you can see it too!**

THE DIVINE NATURE

If all of what has been stated so far is *the cake*, then what we are going to talk about now would have to be *the icing on the cake* - THE DIVINE NATURE! After **Louis** went through **the fire, prayed for truth, saw his position of testimony, looked in the mirror, and knew Who God really was**, God specifically had him to "sit down with the apostle Peter for coffee" and brought his attention to 2nd Peter chapter one concerning the "divine nature". If there was ever a passage of Scripture that cranked his tractor, this was the one. If I heard him talk about the "divine nature" once, I heard him talk about it hundreds of times. He just felt it was that important for us (and God's church in this day and age) to know and understand what Peter (his main man) was talking about. He called it "the recipe for becoming an overcomer".

He did caution me (and himself), though, not to make a denomination out of the "divine nature", just to understand the absolute importance of what it meant to *partake* of the "divine nature". **Louis** also said…"It will bring you from the *wrinkle* to the *twinkle!*" Ephesians 5:27 states…"That He might present it to Himself a glorious church, **not having spot, or wrinkle**, or any such thing; but that it should be holy and without blemish." As well, 1st Corinthians 15:52 states…"In a moment, in **the twinkling of an eye**, at the last trump: for the trumpet shall sound, and the dead shall be raised incorruptible, and we shall be changed." Hence, **Louis** referred to this as *going from the wrinkle to the twinkle*. It would do all of us well to take the time to go down *God's nature trail* and to see what Peter had to say about the "divine nature".

2nd Peter 1:3-11 (King James Version):

3According as **His divine power** has given unto us **all things** that *pertain* **unto life and godliness**, through the **_knowledge_** of Him that has called us to glory and virtue: **4**Whereby are given unto us **exceeding great and precious promises**: that by these you might be **_partakers of the divine nature_**, having escaped the corruption that is in the world through lust. **5**And beside this, **_giving all diligence_**, add to your **faith** virtue; and to **virtue** knowledge; **6**And to **knowledge** temperance; and to **temperance** patience; and to **patience** godliness; **7**And to **godliness** brotherly kindness; and to **brotherly kindness charity**. **8**For if these things be in you, and abound, they make you that you shall neither be barren nor unfruitful in the **_knowledge_** of our Lord Jesus Christ. **9But he that lacks these things is blind, and cannot see afar off**, and has **forgotten that he was purged from his old sins**. **10**Wherefore the rather, brethren, **_give diligence_** to **make your calling and election sure**: for if you do these things, **you shall never fall**: **11**For so **an entrance** shall be ministered unto you abundantly **into the everlasting kingdom** of our Lord and Saviour Jesus Christ.

There is so much that can be said about this passage, but my goal is (as **Louis** would say) to "*bring it on home*" and to "*put the hay down where the goats can eat it*"…if you know what I mean. So…let's try to make this as simple as possible.

Folks…we have a nature problem. It is called the "Adam Nature" (also referred to as the sin nature, the fallen nature, the corrupt nature, or the carnal mind). News flash just in…Jesus Christ (the Lamb of God) has been crucified, buried, and risen again on our behalf. We are to put our faith in Who He is and what He has accomplished on our behalf. The apostle Peter has just told us that what has been accomplished on our behalf is that God has…"given unto us **all things** that *pertain* **unto**

life and godliness, through the _**knowledge**_ of Him that has called us to glory and virtue: Whereby are given unto us **exceeding great and precious promises**: that by these you might be _**partakers of the divine nature**_." THIS IS THE SOLUTION FOR OUR NATURE PROBLEM! THIS IS THE ONLY THING THAT CAN AND WILL REVERSE THE CURSE!

Ask God to reveal to you the _**simplicity**_ that is to be found in this passage. Peter is really not giving us a list of things that we need to try to do, and then we will become like God. Rather, he is telling us (just the opposite) that God has already done something on our behalf and that we are able to access what has been accomplished for us and become a partaker (sharer, participator, partner, and associate) of God's very nature. Peter tells us that…"God by His divine power has given us all things that pertain to life and godliness." You see…this is about what God has done, and that we are to access what has already been done for us. How…through _**knowledge!**_ Think about it! You cannot partake of something you know nothing about. Once again, the passage goes on to tell us God has given us exceeding great and precious promises. Take Him up on His gifts! But how…you ask? The answer is…through _**knowledge!**_

Peter then goes on to tell us of **seven things** that will result from our partaking of the divine nature. They are: **virtue, knowledge, temperance, patience, godliness, brotherly kindness, and charity (love)**. Once God develops these things in you…you shall be…"fruitful in the _**knowledge**_ of the Lord Jesus Christ." We are warned, though, that if these things are not in us we will be…"blind, not see afar off, and will even forget we were purged from our old sins." This is why Peter tells us to "make our calling and election sure: for if you do (bring forth) these things, you shall never fall (stumble)." And finally, we then find ourselves at the entrance of the everlasting kingdom (the Kingdom of the Ages).

After hearing all of this you still may say…"Thomas…I just don't get it. You are making this sound so simple, but I must be missing something, because I don't have what you are speaking of." Listen folks…This is not a quick fix formula that you are going to apply and all of your sin nature is going to be consumed in five minutes. Becoming like the Lord is a process. Remember…we are going from the _wrinkle_ to the _twinkle_. One thing I will tell you is this: You cannot go wrong with **diligence, asking, seeking, knocking, receiving, and partaking**. If you continue in these things **God will do the work of sanctification on you gradually - a little at a time**. If you feel like you do not have _**revelation knowledge**_ of God to partake of, I would encourage you to simply **ASK GOD TO GIVE IT TO YOU!** Read Ephesians 1:17-23, which speaks of the…"spirit of wisdom and revelation in the _**knowledge**_ of Jesus Christ." You may say again…"Yeah…but I don't have revelation in God or this _**knowledge**_ you are talking about." Well…_**ask, seek, and knock with diligence! Diligence is the key!**_ I can promise you that God will reveal Himself to you in the person and work of the Lord Jesus Christ!

**So…in a nutshell, partaking of God's divine nature is to KNOW Who He is, what He has accomplished on our behalf through Jesus Christ, and to BELIEVE it!**

**This is the process whereby God justifies, sanctifies, and glorifies us!**

The amazing part about all of this is that after I was fortunate enough to work with **Louis** for **seven years and seven days**, God put me right back with Norandex Building Materials. They opened up a store in the Baton Rouge area again and hired me back. It was almost as though God sent me on a **seven year journey** to learn these things and then placed me right back where I had left off. My last day at Acoustical Specialties was **08/08/2008**. Sorry for you skeptics out there, but this is no coincidence. We know **seven** is the number of perfection or completion, and **eight** is the number of new beginning. **God sealed up His perfect work He did in me with the confirmation of numbers as well. WOW…is God amazing or what!?**

I thank God that I have been fortunate enough to know "The Man With The Boots"! He truly has gone through the fire of God and put on pure gold - the divine nature! **His story of going through the fire, praying for truth, taking a position of testimony, seeing himself and God in the mirror, and being a partaker of the divine nature is the "recipe for becoming an overcomer" in God's Kingdom!**

My prayer is that this information will take root in your heart, and that you will truly be the overcomer that God has called you to be. My goal (as **Louis Thompson** would say) in writing this was to _"bring it on home"_ to where you (the reader) will grasp **The Greatness Of God!** If you are **diligent** to seek God concerning these matters, He will be faithful to reveal Himself to you and cause you to be a _"can't miss"_ son or daughter of God in His Kingdom! Amen!

Thank you God for sending us…"The Man With The Boots" - **Louis D. Thompson!**

The following people are quoted in this book. The teachings in which they are quoted are listed after their name. If the quote came from a specific book, article, or work it is listed after the quote.

Abbott, Louis: Part 8, Part 9

Adams, A. P.: Part 8, Part 9

Addair, George: Part 6

Allen, Dr.: Part 8

Amirault, Gary: Part 8

Balfour, Walter: Part 9

Beauchemin, Gerry: Part 7

Britton, Bill: Part 7

Campbell, Dr.: Part 8

Chapman, Dr.: Part 8

Eby, J. Preston: Part 8, Part 9

Eckerty, Ken: Part 8

Ellefson, Lloyd: Part 9

Farrar, Canon: Part 8

Firbairn, Dr.: Part 8

Gavazzoni, John: Part 9

Hanson, J. W.: Part 8, Part 9

Hawtin, George: Part 8

Henry, Matthew: Part 4

Jones, Dr. Stephen: Part 1, Part 2, Part 6, Part 9

Le Clere: Part 8

Leigh, Edward: Part 8

Lovelace, Dr. Harold: Part 2, Part 9

Martin, Ernest L.: Part 8

Pridgeon, Charles: Part 9

Prinzing, Ray: Part 9

Reid, C. Gary: Part 8

Roach, Elwin R.: Part 9

S. Ambrose Of Milan: Part 9

Skinner, Otis: Part 9

Stuart, Prof.: Part 8

Thayer, Dr.: Part 8

Thompson, Billy: Part 5

Whitby, Rev. Dr.: Part 8

Zodhiates, Spiros: Part 4

Notes:

ORDER FORM

THE NOBLE BEREAN SERIES VOLUME 3

Send this form, a photocopy of this form or a letter containing the information requested below to:

Straightway Publishing Company
P.O. Box 45212 #261
Baton Rouge, LA. 70895

Enclose a check or money order for $12.95, payable to Straightway Publishing Company. Straightway Publishing Company will pay shipping and handling and any sales taxes.

Fill in name and address where the book is to be shipped:

Name:_____

Address:_____

City:_____ State:_____ Zip:_____

In case of questions concerning your order, please give your phone number and Email address:

Telephone:_____

Email address:_____

If you have any questions, Straightway Publishing Company can be reached by calling (225) 766-0896.

*If this book is unsatisfactory for any reason
you may return it for a full refund.*

http://www.hearingthetruthofgod.com/

www.ingramcontent.com/pod-product-compliance
Lightning Source LLC
Chambersburg PA
CBHW071701040426
42446CB00011B/1857